Opening Hearts by Opening Minds

Opening Hearts by Opening Minds
Reading Fiction That Changes Lives

CONNIE WINELAND

Wipf & Stock
PUBLISHERS
Eugene, Oregon

OPENING HEARTS BY OPENING MINDS
Reading Fiction That Changes Lives

ISBN 13: 978-1-4982-4989-8

*In loving memory of my dad, Richard Eugene Fulks,
who helped instill in me a love for reading and discussing
all types of books, and who taught me that it's okay to question.*

Contents

Acknowledgements

I ESPECIALLY WANT to acknowledge the women who were members of the book club I facilitated for four years. Not only did these women stick it out with me, and read whatever books I chose, their participation and contributions gave back so much more to me than they could ever imagine. I wish to thank all of the following for the great conversations we had and the laughs we shared: Vicki Gilbert, Donna Neff, Francis Spaulding, Barbara Veech, Martha Jean Fleming, Wanda Kitchen, Shirley Ryan, Barbara Davis, Pat Brown, Jerry Barber, Fern Bloemker, Bonnie Shimek, Anna Lois Lewis, Myra Henry, Joyce Verkruyse, and all of the others who came for a short while, or who showed up only once or twice to discuss a particular book. You all kept me on my toes, and kept me going!

I would like to say a special thank you to my husband, John Wineland, for being there on my journey, and for helping me work it out. God put you in my path, and together we've learned of His Grace. Also, thank you for taking me on a pilgrimage to visit the places where Tolkien and Lewis both lived, worked, shared book discussions, and died. It was one part of my life coming full circle.

I would also like to say thank you to my daughter, Christie Lynn McCartney for your love, understanding, and forgiveness. I dragged you through a lot, but you've come out more than okay! I love you!

Finally, there are a few other acknowledgements I need to express. Thank you to Thayer Talbott for introducing me to so many thought-provoking books, and for all the wonderful discussions that have emerged from those readings. You've been with me since graduate school, and even when my path took off in a different direction, you were always there to listen and talk through ideas with me whenever I needed. You are truly a good friend and a blessing.

Also, thank you Connie Swietanski for picking up where my mother left off. Your interest in my life, and your words of encouragement have meant more to me than you know.

And to my sister, Robin. What can I say? You were walking beside me from the beginning. We've shared so much together, and we've found our own ways apart, but through it all we have been each other's friends. Thanks for always being there, and for listening to me through all the stages of my journey.

Introduction

Book clubs and reading groups have been around for a long time, but in recent years, thanks in part to Oprah Winfrey, they have gained in popularity across the United States. They seem to not be bound either by geographic location, or by age, though they are still somewhat defined by gender. What we have learned by Oprah's book club is not only that a recommendation from her will sell millions of books, but that there are still millions of Americans who like to read, and who like to read a book based upon a recommendation from someone they know, or based upon a bestseller list like the one published by the *New York Times*, or even Christian bestseller lists like the one in *Today's Christian Woman* magazine. However, there exists a sentiment that books on some of these lists are sometimes of questionable content and or language. Many people want to read a good book, but feel that finding one is often a risky endeavor, especially if left on their own to browse the many shelves in their local bookstore. If they feel that they have to read ten trashy novels to find one good one, it is a ratio that is too high.

Many times I have found this to be the case in Christian circles concerning fiction published by secular publishing houses, and as a result I have noticed two things. One is that readers who prefer "clean" reading turn to Christian pulp fiction, that is, fiction that is plot driven and formulaic, or two, a person may have come to the conclusion, as I once did, that all that is available by Christian publishing houses often inspires nothing more than a devotional level feel-good response, which in no way would I ever suggest is a bad thing. However, since this is often perceived as the only intended purpose of Christian fiction, some people choose not to read fiction at all. When I taught a course in Christian fiction I was amazed at my students' lack of familiarity with the vast array of Christian fiction that had been written. Also, when I started a Christian Reader's Group this amazement was reinforced by the fact that most of the members of the group were not familiar with many of the titles that I asked them to read. Both my classes and my reader's group have ended up feeling not only deeply gratified that they were exposed to works that were challenging to them spiritually, they were still satisfied that most, if not all of the works they read still maintained in them an element of entertainment.

I decided to do a little informal research in the field of Christian fiction to see why it was that at least the people I had come in contact with professionally had not read as widely in this area as I might have expected. I want to mention here that my experience has been with readers who have ranged in age from eighteen to seventy, and who have been both male and female, though mostly the latter. Because I was not a frequenter of Christian bookstores since I was in the habit of ordering from catalogs, I decided to start there. I have made it a habit over the last several years to visit every Christian bookstore that I have run across, and what I have found to be true for the smaller stores is that usually due to the problem of space, the fiction selection is very limited compared to the shelves of Bibles, theological books, Sunday School aides, music materials, and devotional readers. While what fiction that is on the shelves makes for reading that leaves one with a little bit to chew on, and feeling momentarily uplifted, and though most of it is written in the same caliber of that which is published by secular presses, it is true as well that just like not all secularly published fiction has strong literary elements, not all Christian fiction does either, and thus would not facilitate good classroom or book club discussions. My other observation is that fiction has primarily been thought of as something that women read, and thus does not have to contain provocative material, and that serious readers, especially of theology, read strictly non-fictional works, as they are under the impression that reading anything else would be a waste of time.

Since I believe that there is a massive amount of Christian fiction being neglected by many uninformed Christian readers, and because I believe that if readers knew what books were out there, what they were about, and where to find them their lives would be greatly enriched, I have decided to put together a book that I wished would have been available when I started reading and researching in the field of Christian fiction. In writing this book, I discovered that there are several books already on the market that have been written for readers groups, and I have listed most of them in my selected bibliography, but not one book group book has, as of yet, addressed Christian readers. I personally believe that Christian-based reading groups could become very popular as alternative programming for small group ministries.[1] I believe that a Christian reader's group can serve as an evangelistic outreach as well. I also believe that a book such as this could be a helpful resource for any individual who would like a ready-made list of good literature to read. It could also be used as a cur-

1. Wineland, Connie. "Opening Hearts by Opening Books." *The Lookout* 112:46 (Nov. 12, 2000) 3.

riculum source for home schoolers or other Christian educators. It is my hope that this book not only answers the question "Why read fiction," but also explains more thoroughly what Christian fiction is, or rather, what it can be. I have included the story of my own arduous spiritual journey to conversion to Christianity by way of Buddhism, New Age religions, and literary study. Following that is a list of annotated book titles from my own personal library, many of which were instrumental to my growth after my conversion. There are also three nine-month sample syllabi with thirty-four discussion guides for anyone interested in starting a more literary and spiritually based reader's group of their own. There is at the end a glossary of literary terms to further aid readers' understanding of various literary terms and genres, and a list of resources useful for ordering books, for obtaining reviews of books, and a list of a few other potentially useful Internet addresses. Following that there is a bibliography of non-fictional works that I found very useful; I recommend the books listed there to you if you are interested in reading more deeply into this subject. It is with the greatest enthusiasm and love for reading Christian fiction that I have written this book. I hope that my quest for good books will help open up to readers a world richer than anyone might have otherwise imagined in this life.

1

Why Read Fiction?

THIS WOULD certainly sound like an idiotic question if you were answering it in regards to a child, but it becomes more legitimate when you are answering it in terms of why an adult should read fiction. It becomes even more legitimate when that adult is considering theological matters, which on the surface would seem to require serious reading of the Scriptures and other non-fictional texts only. The reason I pose the question in general terms instead of specifically asking "Why read *Christian* fiction?" is because many of the reasons for reading any type of fiction would be the same, and because after answering the first question, *why read fiction*, it is then that we may proceed to the specific nature of Christian fiction, and what, if anything, distinguishes it as a separate genre. And the reason I pose the question at all to an audience to whom this is probably a moot point, is because I know from personal experience that I have had to defend the answer to this on more than one occasion. The first time I had to was when I announced to my family my decision to major in English. My personal reasoning behind my choice of a major was because I liked to read more than do anything else, but of course I had to have a better answer than that when it became clear that I did not intend to major in Education and become a high school English teacher. Their assumption was that besides becoming familiar with a large body of literature, I wouldn't learn anything that would truly benefit me in a future career. Since then I have had to address this issue for a countless number of college students who have been forced, as they saw it, to take a literature class.

I usually begin by asking exactly what is the power of fiction that we believe in it so absolutely when we are young, and when we are parents of young ones? Most of us know that fictional stories have elements of universal truths encased in them, so that making up characters or settings makes no difference to the truth that is being told. We all know that Jesus told stories. In fact, much of what He spoke of when he was teaching his disciples lessons that have made up the Gospels was told as parables, or stories. Stories tend to reach us as listeners and readers through our hearts.

A textbook can give us facts to remember, to weigh and to digest, but most of us are moved far more readily when something touches our heart. This is why ministers often tell stories as part of their sermons. They know the power that a story can wield on the hearts of their listeners. This is why we tell our young children bible "stories." We are not so afraid that they may not be getting all the facts and the proper theology, because we know that they are getting truths in a form that they can understand, and that all truths emanate from God. I don't believe that Christ was a theologian in the sense of the word as what we know it to mean today. I believe that He taught theology, but that He put it in a form so that even the simplest minded could understand it. In fact, the Bible is full of poetry, and letters, and songs, all speaking the language of truth, all speaking to our hearts, and yet they are all types of writing that any "scholar" today would most likely shun as a way to teach anything that "really" mattered.

But beyond encasing historical truths about mankind and the universe, what else do we as adults value about fiction when it comes to children reading it? Of course we want our children to develop language skills, and so we allow for reading of almost anything in hopes that our children will be better speakers and writers. But what else do children get from reading besides that? What effect does reading have on their imaginations, and on their belief systems? Do you remember when you read fairytales? You did not have to be told that there was no such thing as talking animals and trees, or dragons, and elves and goblins, or big bad wolves that ate unsuspecting grandmothers. Okay, you might have had to be told that there was no such real place as Narnia, or Middle Earth, or Oz, if you were young enough, but instead of being disgusted and refusing to ever read another fictional work again, you were more likely regretful, and disappointed, but eager to find another wonderful place where laws of gravity and time didn't apply. Or a place where the sky was green and the land blue, and where animals talked, and people could fly. You would have probably been very eager to visit a realm where you could know for certain who were the bad guys and who were the good guys (although many times they would often be disguised as their opposites at first), and a place where good would always win, though there would definitely be physical, emotional, and/or moral struggles. And beyond that, reading with our children gives us a chance to teach them how to discuss what they read. Many times as parents we sit down with our children and reflect together on what they just read, and then we lead them into more abstract thinking, or personal or moral application. However, there are some people who do not believe that reading fictional works too long into childhood, and especially into adulthood, is good for a person. There are parents who would wean their children off of such books, and guide them towards more realistic types of stories, hoping that they would eventually quit reading fiction altogether. I suppose that the danger I see in this is that God created us in His image, and part of being like God is having an imagination and the desire ourselves to be creators of sorts. When we stifle our imaginations, we deny that part of the godhood that lives in us. We as Christians believe that God is creating for us a new heaven and a new earth, and we in part believe that there will be things created for us that we are maybe not able to imagine as yet. And we know that creating is one of God's greatest pleasures, and yet we live in a world where the creative mind and the strongly developed imagination are not encouraged because we have bought into the idea that anyone with an "overly active imagination," or too much of a creative bent could not easily function or get along in this world of required conformity, and use of limited or repetitive skills. And so we discourage it in all its forms as much as possible, unless we believe that money can definitely be made from a particular creative endeavor. Even allowing children to play computer games for long periods of time, while teaching them hand-eye coordination, zaps their creativity. If the child grows up and wants to become a computer game designer, it will require both skill and imagination to create a new game that will keep the interest of the children of the next generation, who will require more visual stimulation and more action.

But putting the endeavor of making money aside, there is yet another reason for why developing an imagination of any kind, and opening our hearts to a possible reality of any kind other than the one we live in would be beneficial, and that has to do with faith. The language of faith is the language of the heart. In order to be able to believe the story of Christ's incarnation and resurrection one finally has to have the ability to believe that what would seem like pure fiction is in fact truth. In order for us to believe stories about angels sitting around the throne of God and doing His work, and acting as His messengers, or even to believe stories about demons and their powers, we have to have an active and receptive imagination! In order for us to listen to Christ we have to have open and ready hearts, hearts that will recognize truth in story form. We know that the Bible is like a mirror, that when we read it we often glean different insights from it, depending on where we are in our lives, and what is going on in them. We know that the Bible cannot be read only with one's intellect, though we never want to undervalue that, ever. But reading without an open heart can be just as disastrous. We know that we are to look to the Bible as the Word of God, and that God teaches us through circumstances, and through other people, and even through other venues. But we also need to understand that unless we reflect on the things that happen in our lives, we will gain very little, if any insight, and thus will grow very little spiritually. If we read the Bible, and yet do not reflect on what we read, we will not grow. Of course the act of reflection is an intellectual endeavor, but coexisting with the intellect as a part of that endeavor is the act of using our hearts to yield to the lesson, either in humility, or in gladness, or in any other emotion. Even when I teach critical thinking skills to college students in my writing and literature classes I sometimes wonder if I am possibly doing them a disservice in so far as they may become less naïve and less compliant, wanting to question more of what is presented to them, either in class, on the job, or in life. But ideally, isn't that what we want? Plus, thinking critically is a skill that teaches individuals to approach all subjects and problems that present themselves in life with a broader perspective. And one of the easiest tools for teaching critical thinking skills is literature. Reading, then, even if it is a work of fiction, becomes a spiritual act if we read both critically and reflectively. I believe that all of this, our hearts, our minds, and our spirits, is tied up in the matter of faith.

Fiction can also speak what we feel. We do not as humans have to personally experience everything, but we can, through reading, share in the experiences of people different from us, and who are from lands different from ours, and who may even be from times that are different from our present time. We can share in their struggles, their hopes and their dreams; we can learn that we are not that different in our humanness from other people, and we can continue to define and examine ourselves by the characters that we read about in terms of their reactions to and interactions with their "life" circumstances. We know that Christ understood our weaknesses, though He did not have to experience our failures. We know that He commanded us to love God, and to love our neighbor as ourselves. Reading about people living lives that we may never live and thus may never understand, looking at them in terms of what motivated them to act in certain ways, what their weaknesses were and what caused them hurt, and what their strengths were and what were their rewards and why, is a good way to open up our hearts to people who are different from us. Thus we may be more readily able to love different people when we meet them in real life. I believe that reading fiction plays a strong role in helping us to do just that, if we do not use it as a form of escapism. Anything that God can use to enrich and expand people's lives can also be used as a tool to distort and destroy. This being the case may be the number one reason that Christians throughout history have predominately chosen to avoid works of fiction. There has often been a general belief among conservative Christians that fiction is indeed nothing more than a form of escapism, or that it is just so much trash. This fear of books has also been precipitated by the fear of obscenity, profanity, depravity, and perversion that many Christians suspect is lurking behind the pages of secular fiction. However, any good work of literature, even fiction, has the power to strip us naked to the point where truth can be felt and seen! It can bring us into honest confrontation with ourselves, much like a mirror. We don't have to limit our seeing and understanding to the Scriptures only, but we can look into the entire world of fiction, which at first may seem like an escape *from* reality, but which in all its power to reach one's heart will eventually bring a person face to face *with* reality!

2

What is Christian Fiction?

T HE FIRST time I tried to answer this question seriously was when I began teaching at a Christian college and was asked to teach a course in Christian literature. Since it was going to fulfill the literature requirement for several majors, I wanted the course to be as thought - provoking and challenging as any other literature course. At that time my background in that area of literature was limited to what I knew of the fiction titles listed in the Christian Book Distributors (CBD) catalog, and from my already extensive reading of everything by C. S. Lewis. However, that first semester I did not want to teach a course strictly using the works of Lewis, though later on I did. But what I wanted was to stretch my students and myself by exploring a variety of authors, both contemporary and historical, and to read in a variety of genres. To this end I decided to call on the help of a very good friend who was teaching at John Brown University in Arkansas. I asked him what he would include on a syllabus for a Christian literature course. As it turned out, another professor there had taught a course in Christian literature, and so she was kind enough to e-mail me a list of works that she had used. After looking it over I realized that she had been thinking about Christian literature as existing within a larger framework than what I was considering, and thus I began my quest to find an answer to the question, just what does define literature as being "Christian"?

Research into several books on the subject resulted in the conclusion that by definition it would have to be any literature that contained or supported a Christian perspective, or worldview. This definition does not always mean, however, that a work has to be overtly Christian. I remember the academic dean of the Christian college where I worked telling me that her rule of thumb was that any topic that was in the Bible (and try to find anything that is not discussed in there!) was acceptable in a literary work as long as sinful lifestyles were not being glorified or excused as right behavior, or thrown in for strictly entertainment purposes! She also included in that rule the use of cuss words and profanity for entertainment purposes. Unfortunately, it was in that environment that students in one of my composition classes refused to read *Zen and the Art of Motorcycle Maintenance* by Robert Pirsig because it contained language they found offensive. Written in 1974, it is a book about perception, reality, and values; it's about learning to look at yourself and life differently, and incorporates into its context numerous references to Plato's *Phaedrus*. The dean requested that I give her a count of the number of potentially offensive words, whereupon she would make the decision as to whether the percentage based on the total page count of 377 was too high. It was. Interestingly though, all but one of those same students had recently gone to see *Dangerous Minds*, a movie rated R for language about an English teacher in an inner-city high school who taught delinquents. While I learned through this experience that I myself had become desensitized to the use of "offensive" language, I also realized that those students' righteous indignations were based on values other than refusal to fill their minds with words that offended them! It was being used as an excuse not to read! Had we made it through Pirsig's book, we could have had a thought-provoking discussion of how one determines what is or is not of value, or rather what is or is not good. Another time I remember someone being upset by a book I chose was when a wife of one of our older students told me that she had trusted my judgment as to what was good, clean Christian reading, and so bought a book I was using in one of my courses to read on her own. She related to me that she was not able to make it through such a disgusting book, and was so upset by it that she flung it across her living room. The book was Maya Angelou's *I Know Why the Caged Bird Sings*. Thankfully my class of predominately Afro-American (and Christian) female students did not share her same feelings! Angelou's description of the childhood rape scene was an act of empowerment, of giving voice to her pain after having lived seven years of her childhood after that incident in silence. It's a story that Maya Angelou has shared with millions, who find in her words the capacity for healing!

Unfortunately, there has been a long history of censorship of literature in America, as well as around the world, not only for religious reasons, but for political and social reasons as well. Many of the books included on the banned book list might astound even the most conservative Christian reader. For example, *Uncle Tom's Cabin* was banned for challenging mainstream Christianity's acceptance of slavery, for suggesting that it might be more Christian to go against the Fugitive Slave Law, and for making black characters more virtuous than their white counterparts. So, while it is an extremely pro-Christian novel, it upset the church and the clergy for many reasons. Books like Mark Twain's *Adventures of Huckleberry Finn*, and Harper Lee's *To Kill a Mockingbird* have been protested against due to racism and language. John Steinbeck's *The Grapes of Wrath* was banned almost immediately for reasons of indecency, obscenity, and for its degrading portrayal of people and life. Even *Oliver Twist,* by Charles Dickens, was protested as being anti-Semitic for referring to the character of Fagin as "the Jew." However, it has been argued that Dickens did not intend to defame or injure Jews, but that he was a product of an 1830s anti-Semitic culture. The list of censored books, which includes non-fiction as well as fiction, is quite lengthy. My point is that it is difficult to be the consummate judge of what constitutes good Christian reading.

What I knew from my studies in American literature (and British and any other world literature for that matter) was that historically, any author who wrote during a time when the culture in which he lived was predominately Christian, would have been influenced by Christian thought, whether he agreed with it or not. Therefore, there was almost always a strong sense of morality, and standards of decency, and thus whenever authors were not idealizing man's behavior, they would have been critical of his immorality, oftentimes satirizing man's religious hypocrisy. When people began to question the Church during the Renaissance period, and eventually even Christianity itself, as well as the belief in a Judeo-Christian God, which happened during what is called the Age of Reason, or the Enlightenment period, is when the idea of a Creator was no longer going to be taken for granted by the majority of educated writers. This could especially be demarcated in literature after the publication in 1859 of Darwin's *Origin of Species,* probably the most influential non-Christian work ever published, which strongly put forth the theory of evolution. Before this, American authors for example, who had not ever considered themselves to be Christian, like Louisa May Alcott, Benjamin Franklin, and Emerson and Thoreau were still strongly influenced by Christianity. For example, many people have mistakenly quoted Ben Franklin when they thought they were quoting Proverbs, that was how influenced by his culture he was. Even though he was a Deist, he could neither escape the influence of the strong Puritan work ethic, or some of the ideas enveloped in the movement of The Great Awakening. Many other writers came from families who had preachers related to them somehow. It cannot be overstated that it is the families who came from educated and literate backgrounds who often produced writers, and that their educations came primarily from religious institutions of higher learning.

Looking at it this way, many authors who wrote before 1859 could be included in a Christian literature reading list, and many who wrote even another hundred years after 1859 could be included. However, two critical literary movements, which began in the late nineteenth century, changed the face of literature. The first, known as Naturalism, which followed on the heels of Darwin, held that a human being belongs entirely in the order of nature and does not have a soul or any other mode of participation in a religious or spiritual world beyond nature, and thus character and fortunes are determined by heredity and environment. Naturalistic writers, which included Americans Frank Norris, Stephen Crane, and Theodore Drieser, often portrayed characters who exhibited strong animal drives such as greed and sexual desire, and who were victims both of their hormonal urges from within, and of sociological pressures from without. Their works exhibited social Darwinism, or survival of the fittest. Characters would do whatever it took to survive, or else risk falling into ruin or death. Realism, the other late nineteenth century literary theory, was a movement to represent human life and experience in literature as an actual imitation of life as it is, as opposed to romantic fiction which presented life more as we would have it to be, that is, more picturesque, more adventurous, more heroic than the actual. The Romantic Period followed the Age of Reason in the eighteenth century, and is often seen as a reaction against the Enlightenment and the rise of industrialism. It most often represented a return to nature and religion, though in a more mystical form. There was also much more attention put on feeling[1], intuition, and imagination. It produced poets such as Blake, Coleridge, Keats, Byron, and Walt Whitman; and novelists and essayists such as Washington Irving, James Fennimore Cooper, Ralph Waldo Emerson, Henry David Thoreau, and Herman Melville. Out of this movement arose the Gothic novel, where not only was attention paid to the supernatural and eerie, but it dealt with emotional extremes and dark themes, such as the grotesque and terrors of the soul. Works included villainous, evil, mad, or demonic stock characters. Gothic writers included Mary Shelley (*Frankenstein*), Edgar Allan Poe (*Fall of the House of Usher* and *The Tell-Tale Heart*), Emily Bronte (*Wuthering Heights*), Nathaniel Hawthorne (*Young Goodman Brown*, *The Minister's Black Veil*, and *The House of the Seven Gables*), Robert Louis Stevenson (*Dr. Jekyll and Mr. Hyde*), Oscar Wilde (*The Picture of Dorian Gray*), and Bram Stoker (*Dracula*)[2]. These kinds of works clearly remind us that man has a dark side, and that evil does exist. It is also during the Romantic Period where the idea of nationalism evolves, which produced writers who wrote stories

---

1. It is from the evolution of the novel of the Romantic Period (plus our Medieval concept of chivalry and courtly love) that we get our modern concept of the romance novel.

2. Stoker also establishes Transylvania, located in Romania, as the center of the Gothic movement in Europe.

that try to preserve the heritage of Germany by telling folktales that they collected from local country peasants. Realism, on the other hand, involved rendering a subject in such a way as to give the reader the illusion of actual and ordinary experience. That included portraying the seedier sides of life and of human nature, most often without hope and without a happy ending. After the Civil War, and up until the turn of the century, there began to be an expansion in population due to immigration, and a rise of the middle class due to industrialization, as well as increased literacy. Writers became interested in exploring and representing the effects of these rapid changes on man and society. Characters are revealed in their real temperaments and motives, with an emphasis on the middle and lower classes, and diction is now in the natural vernacular. Interior, or psychological realism is also beginning to be revealed. Writers in this movement are most notably William Dean Howells, Rebecca Harding Davis, Henry James, and Mark Twain, and regionalist writers such as Willa Cather and Kate Chopin.

After World War I critics began to break with some of the traditional bases of Western culture and of Western art. Intellectual precursors of the movement, termed as "modernism," were thinkers who questioned traditions that supported modes of social organization, religion, morality, and the conception of the human self. This again changed the face of literature. Writers such as Karl Marx, Sigmund Freud, and Frederick Nietzsche stressed the correspondence between central Christian tenets and pagan myths and rituals. World War I seemed to shake men's faith in the foundations and continuity of Western civilization and culture. Finally, the term "post modernism" has been applied to the literature and art after World War II. World War II had disastrous effects on Western morale when we experienced Nazi totalitarianism and mass extermination, the threat of total destruction by the atomic bomb, the progressive devastation of the natural environment, and the ominous fact of overpopulation and starvation. Postmodernism took modernism to its extreme and beyond to subvert the foundations of our accepted modes of thought and experience to reveal the "meaninglessness" of existence and the underlying "abyss," or "nothingness" on which our supposed security is precariously suspended. Within postmodernism there has been an effort to subvert the foundations of language itself, so as to show that words are meaningless, and thus arbitrary. That is one reason why there is so much profanity in the arts today. However, it usually happens only in retrospect that critics can look back and mark an event or period of time as when a new movement began, in part because changes in society take place, or evolve, more slowly than in the more progresive and reflective thinking of the higher arts and philosophy.

Thus, it wasn't until sometime after WWII, several decades, in fact, that a Christian reaction to postmodern theory popped up, and we saw developing a market specifically for "Christian" literature, and that has been in part an evangelical response to an overall acceptance by a majority of non-Christians in the theory of evolution and relativism by people who would define themselves as intellectuals and artists. Thinking either that no God could exist who would let all this suffering happen, or else just unable to accept that what was really wrong with the world was that mankind needed a Savior, writers either threw God out altogether, or else a turned to Eastern or pagan forms of spirituality. Now, what we have today in terms of what is being labeled "Christian," and what has become a very prosperous market, rose out of the evangelical movement, which has regretfully been predominately white, and really didn't come into full maturity until sometime during the 1980s. Remember, before the latter half of the twentieth century there was no such particular designation, and it is still not recognized as a legitimate academic area of study in secular colleges and universities. However, as a culture, the West is still hanging on to a dominate Christian worldview, though some would have us believe otherwise, and even within the secular presses one can still find literature with religious frameworks, references, images, metaphors, motifs, and symbols, all fodder for great literary discussions. And as far as what is now specifically labeled as Christian literature, it ought *not* to shelter us from the world and its views, but should challenge us to critically examine what is going on in the world, as well as what is going on in our own lives and within the Church, while offering us hope and a solution.

3

How Reading Changed My Life

IN 1991, at the age of thirty-two, after a very long and sinuous journey, I converted to Christianity. Having reached a point where I was finally humble enough to accept that what Christ did for me and all of humanity was indeed an act of love so grand and so necessary that only God could do it, and that it had in fact truly happened, I would never be able to guess how God would take this previously prodigal daughter and use her in His Church. I had so much to regret, and I knew that it was taking more than a small amount of Grace to cover my sins. I had spent most of my life seeking for truth, and yet, at that freaky moment (as I like to call it) when I could see it right in front of my nose, I'd like to say that I had some holy experience, that I felt a sense of deep peace, or something! However, within only a few moments, that person in me who had been a long time cynic, and who had not yet been redeemed, wanted to scream out, "You've got to be kidding!" I was going to have to learn to love a people who I had for most of my life felt nothing for but distain, and I wasn't at all sure I would be up for the task! But God had his plan, and I ended up married to a man with a M.A. degree from a seminary in Near Eastern Archaeology, a M.Div. in Theology and Christian apologetics, and a Ph.D. in ancient history. After we both graduated from Miami University we took jobs at an extremely conservative small Christian college in a small town in North Carolina located along the coast. After three years there we moved to Kentucky where we would teach at yet another Christian college. Though it would be less conservative, I still found it to be challenging. (Only a few years earlier I would have blamed it on karma!) Alas, on any hero's journey, which must begin with a fool, the quest is only one part of the story. But I'm getting ahead of myself. This is the story of how all that came about.

I have come to learn that most people who exhibit extremely strong feelings against Christianity and Christians have had some connection to it, usually earlier in their lives. This could be said of me too. I was born to parents who were not churchgoers. My dad had grown up in a home with a mother who was a Baptist, but while she encouraged all three of her sons to attend church, they went sporadically at best. However, the two oldest sons as adults remained close to the church, but my dad journeyed in a different direction when he married his high school sweetheart, a spoiled only child who had no religious affiliations whatsoever. Although they did have a beautiful church wedding, never once did they step foot inside that or any other church building again for many decades to come. By the time I was born my parents were having troubles in their marriage, and were seriously considering divorce. However, it was the 1950s and couples back then stuck it out a little longer, and so did my parents, who had a baby boy nineteen months after I was born. That baby made three. Still, all was not well, but my grandfather, my mother's dad, continued to spoil my mother with gifts, purchasing all the home furnishings, appliances, clothes for her and us, and anything else that she wanted. Unfortunately, when I was two he died, and that was the end of that. This caused an emotional and psychological crisis that almost did my parents in, when one day my father heard a radio program that changed the course of their lives and set the course of mine.

Herbert W. Armstrong was Chancellor of Ambassador College in Pasadena, California, and the leader of what was then known as The Radio Church of God[1]. Armstrong had come out of a Seventh Day Adventist background, when he decided, with his wife's encouragement, to start his own church, originally in Oregon, in 1933. It was basically an Old Testament, old covenant religion, stressing the importance of observing the Sabbath and Jewish Holy Days, as well as the importance of following strict dietary laws which distinguished between eating clean and unclean meats, and obeying the tithing laws, which required giving ten percent of your yearly income to the church, saving another ten percent, to be used for feast and holy days, and sending a third ten percent tithe every third year to the headquarters church, which would further test the faith of approximately 30,000 plus converts, and prove God's faith to his people. Furthermore, the church did not believe in taking medicines, getting vaccinations, or going to doctors. God was the Great Healer, and believers had to be healed by their faith and by the laying on of hands. They believed it was wrong to say the pledge of allegiance, to serve in the military, and that all government was

---

1. Later its name was changed to The Worldwide Church of God, which in 1995 became more mainstream evangelical. The people who still held to the original beliefs splintered off into The Living Church of God, and The United Church of God.

suspect. Believers were forbidden to observe Christmas, Easter, Valentine's Day, Halloween, or anyone's birthday, as these all had pagan origins. Most importantly, the church professed that they were the one and only true church, and that all other religions, Catholic and Protestant alike, were wrong and Satanic, and all but members of the Worldwide Church of God were doomed to burn in hell. However, even being a member of the true church did not automatically guarantee anyone a place in the kingdom. We heard loads of sermons warning us against being spiritually lukewarm, and on the necessity of always obeying God in word, thought, and deed, lest we end up in the fires of hell ourselves! God worked through one man at a time, and Herbert W. Armstrong was his modern day prophet, and *he* would keep us on the true but narrow path. However, no outsider listening to just that radio program alone would learn about any of these "doctrinal" beliefs, nor would they read about them in *The Plain Truth*, a slick monthly magazine published by the Ambassador College Press. What initially attracted people to this church, and what definitely attracted my dad, was their belief in building strong families, with fathers at the head, having submissive wives, and well-disciplined children. And they believed that divorce was absolutely wrong! Most likely, that alone gave my father the hope he needed to save the marriage he so desperately wanted to save. All he had to do was convince my mother, which he eventually did. That was late 1961.

And so I grew up indoctrinated into the Worldwide Church of God (WCG). My parents, who began attending a congregation a five-hour drive away in Cincinnati, Ohio, eventually became church leaders, participating in the planting of church congregations in southeastern Ohio, and in West Virginia. My father was ordained as a Preaching Elder by Garner Ted Armstrong, and my mother was ordained a deaconess. Our family not only survived in tact, but also became, well, the "ideal." Constantly reminded by the Armstrongs of the need to be spiritually zealous, lest we not be spared from the great tribulation and the "Lake of Fire," we tithed, fasted, and lived in fear and anticipation that the end times would soon be upon us (first in 1972, then in 1975). Not only were we required to be able to give an answer to anyone who asked about our beliefs (and my parents drilled us kids on church doctrine), we were to stand ready to sell all our belongings, and send all the money to Pasadena, when jets would be purchased for us to leave for the "place of safety" in Petra, Jordan. Supposedly we would stay there protected for 3 ½ years, being fed on manna and water, which would spring miraculously from the rocks. God would seal the wombs of married women, and heal the sick so that all would go smoothly during that time. Not allowing for anything less than an unwavering faith, we never questioned any of this; it would pepper all our conversations, and affect how we lived our daily lives. The shortest trip we ever made to attend church services took us forty-five minutes, but mostly we drove one hour or more one-way to attend services that would last two hours. As children, we would need to ask permission to be exempted from all school holiday observances, which mostly meant no parties, no watching Christmas films, or exchanging valentines; we couldn't even wear green on Saint Patrick's Day; and no coloring Santas, or jack-o-lanterns, or Easter bunnies or eggs (though pumpkins, snowmen, and anything having to do with Thanksgiving or the seasons were okay). In fact, I literally grew up scared to death of Santa Claus whenever I'd see him, who I put in the same category as demons, which I also vehemently feared. (I also feared Catholic churches and Pentecostal churches. However, I did believe that angels were watching over and protecting us from harm and evil.)

One thing we all planned for and looked forward to with great excitement was being taken out of school for two weeks every fall for the Feast of Tabernacles, when we would travel usually to Georgia or Pennsylvania, stay in hotels, eat out, and get a few special gifts. Each spring we would all help Mom clean out every last miniscule crumb of bread and leavening (things that contained yeast) in our house and car in order that we could understand how difficult it was to get rid of sin in our lives. For one whole week we would eat Matzo crackers in observance of the Feast of Unleavened Bread. Never would we eat pork or any seafood other than fish with scales, and never would we break the Sabbath by attending school functions, watching television, or doing any type of chores. One thing I can say is that my parents never lived hypocritically, and my brother, sister, and I rarely misbehaved, and never rebelled, even though we had very strict parents. (I should say here that our mother was much more the disciplinarian than our father, although no one would have guessed it.) Our religion was not something we practiced from sunset Friday to sunset Saturday; it was our whole way of being and existing in the world! And while we lived in the world, we were never to be *of* the world. Needless to say, holding to such strict and unusual religious beliefs made my siblings and I stand out in school. While we were popular among our church family and friends, made even more so because of our family's position in the church, we were oddballs in our small hometown. I usually told teachers and kids at school that my family was Jewish. This seemed easier to me for some reason. I guess I felt more validated by saying I belonged to a recognized religion that had existed for several thousand years! At least everyone had heard of it. (There were no Jews in our town, nor was there anyone who seemed to know anything about Jewish culture or religion, which meant I was never contested on this matter.) I did have one very close Methodist girlfriend from school that I earnestly tried to convert, though to no avail. She was my best friend, and I basically spent all of my non-Sabbath hours with her, though I sometimes did get permission to drag her along to a few of our church socials. I have since apologized to her profusely for the whole business, and we remain friends to this day!

When the world did not come to an end in 1975, many church congregants and leaders began to question some of their doctrines. My own dad, who loved to read and study the Bible and concordances, began to read outside the prescribed church literature and commentaries. He began to understand that some of what he had believed to be true was, in fact, not. When he asked to be released from preaching, he explained that he was beginning to have questions about a few doctrines that the church taught. While he was by no means ready to quit the church, he was immediately excommunicated from it for fear that he would spread heretical beliefs among the other church members. Many leaders at that time were also being excommunicated, and all their names were put on a list, which was circulated throughout the country. What this meant was that no one was to speak to you, or have anything to do with you. And of course, it was assumed that all these men were in the stronghold of Satan. Wives and children were told to separate from their husbands and fathers, and stay true to the church. However, I personally never heard of any wives leaving their husbands for leaving the church.

It was, however, in that same year when Herbert W. Armstrong decided that the church would accept the doctrine of divorce! I assume this had more to do with all the excommunications, but even before Dad was ex-communicated, my parents were first in line to get divorced! My mother wanted it, not my dad, and in retrospect, I guess she felt that she had had to make too many adjustments to her life, emotionally and psychologically becoming someone she was not. Besides, she and Dad had two very different personalities. He more naturally took to law and order, while she longed for less structure and more freedom. But at age 16, I couldn't understand all this; I felt then like I had lost everything. I lost all my church friends, and I was losing my family. By the time all this happened in 1975, my sister was a freshman at Ambassador College in Pasadena. When Mom moved out of the house, she also moved to Pasadena, which was close to where many of her aunts and cousins, and grandmother lived. My brother, who was fourteen, and I both stayed with Dad in West Virginia, though we moved to a new town and had to start at a new school. In 1976 Dad got remarried to a woman from Washington state who was also from the WCG. After corresponding with her through letters, Dad sent for her and her ten-year-old adopted daughter, and after spending one week together, they got married. During that year I suffered a nervous breakdown, and my brother ran away from home. While that marriage only lasted one year, my brother and I both ended up living in California, though my brother would run away again to New York City, where he would be raped while living at the Y.M.C.A. He eventually came out of the closet to live a gay lifestyle, though he lived hard and fast. He had his own story to tell, but before he could he died from AIDS in 1996. My life took a different turn.

I moved out to Pasadena, stayed there for a few months until my dad got a divorce, and then moved back out there again right after I graduated from high school, as he had remarried for a second time. Changes seemed to be taking place all around me. My sister had met a guy from Nebraska at college who had also grown up in the WCG. They were engaged, and after getting married would soon move back to Nebraska. My mother, who was working full time at J. C. Penny, was dating several men all at once, and had taken up chain-smoking cigarettes, and wearing heavy makeup, neither of which had been allowed by the church. I couldn't help but wonder who the woman was who had taken over my mother's body! My dad had newly married a woman from a Protestant background, had started working on Saturdays, and was eating pork, most of which I could accept. But having happened all within a relatively short time, it seemed like a bit much to take in! The parents who had raised me were definitely gone. When I had lived with Dad I was able to virtually come and go as I pleased; he never questioned me as to my comings or goings, as he had been busy himself dating. And so I began to test the waters and break rules that had previously kept me in line.

Ironically, it was that same year, in 1977, the year I graduated from high school, but before I moved to California, that I began to be interested in Catholicism. I had a new best friend who was Catholic, though I think what primarily attracted me to it was that I had been told my whole life that the Catholic Church was the Mother Harlot Church talked about in the Book of Revelations. I had grown up fearing that church more than anything, and would even cross the street so as not to be pulled in by the demons that I believed lurked inside and out of it! Now, partially out of a newfound sense of rebellion against everything I had ever been told, and since I was fast learning that so much of it had been wrong, I decided to enroll in a catechism class. You can only imagine what an ex-WCG p-k had to ask a Catholic priest! However, that kind and patient old priest broke down my defenses so that I really didn't feel like arguing with him all that much, plus the way he explained everything, it seemed to make pretty good sense. In fact, I learned that the Holy Spirit was part of the Trinity of God, which had been denied by my previous church. I learned that souls did not sleep after death, but went to heaven immediately to dwell with the saints. I learned why it was that we did not have to observe a Sabbath, but went to church on Sundays, and how it was that Christmas and Easter could be Christian, observing my first Christmas ever in 1976! I particularly loved the elaborately ornamented church building of St. Francis Xavier, where I had recently begun to visit on breaks from work, just to feel comforted and closer to God. (The WCG never built or owned buildings-they always rented halls.) I was also attracted to the rich history of the church, and how so much seemed to be shrouded in mystery instead of legalism. I was enthralled with the symbolism, the candles lit as prayers, the rosary, the myriad of saints, the liturgy, and the overall atmosphere of reverence and holiness. Father Scanlon explained to me how Peter had been the first "Pope," and how the church developed and grew from there. I felt comfortable calling him "father," and crossing myself with holy water and kneeling upon entering the nave before the Eucharist at the altar in the Sanctuary. It seemed to fill my very dry soul with something I desperately needed. And so after several months I decided to convert! I took the name "Marie," asked a couple to be my godparents, and was baptized on July 3, 1977. (I had never been baptized in the WCG, as they would only baptize adults. Also, they baptized by immersion, and for the purpose of making you a member of that church.) I was a Catholic, a member of the universal church, a long established church that had millions and millions of believers! I quickly bought myself my first religious jewelry to celebrate—a silver cross and a St. Christopher medallion!

After I moved to California, I tried my best to be a good Catholic, but since absolutely no one I was friends with out there was a practicing Catholic, or Protestant for that matter, and because the WCG headquarters' church was in Pasadena where I was living, which emanated a cloud of oppression that hovered over and darkened my spirit, it was improbable that any new religion for me would last very long. I was carrying too much baggage from my years spent in the WCG. I was screwing up royally, rarely going to church or making confessions, and so the whole thing just went downhill. In less than a year I let go of Catholicism, though I am happy to say that not only did I lose my fear of that church, I learned to love and understand its believers. Very soon though, in 1978, when I was nineteen, I decided to marry the brother of a girl I worked with at the Bank of America Credit Card Center, and while I was not in love, I desperately felt like I needed someone to take care of me. He was four years older than me, in the navy, and stationed in Long Beach. He was not religious, and I would stop being, at least for a good many years.

I have read that it is very difficult for anyone who leaves a cult religion to ever rejoin any other organized form of religion, in part because members are so brainwashed into believing that their church contained the only truth, so that even if they are no longer fully able to accept all that it taught, they most likely are not able to accept that anyone else could be right. This theory has basically proven correct in regards to other members of my family. However, there was a little seed of belief existing in the core of my being that felt that if there were a God, there had to be an absolute Truth. I held that thought in my heart, believing that someday I would get to the bottom of it, that I would search until I found it. However, for now, I needed to take a break and live my life. But, like my bout with Catholicism, my marriage was also doomed to fail. I needed to recover and heal, and I couldn't do that trying to be married to someone I barely knew and didn't love. Being in the navy meant that he had at that time easy access to lots of different drugs. He was a regular user, and I began using a little just so I could dull the pain of unhappiness that I felt. After several months, though, I discovered that I was pregnant, which seemed to be the news I needed to jolt me into questioning what I wanted for my future and the future of my child. What I didn't want was to be married to him and live the life we seemed to be living, and so I filed for divorce and took back my maiden name. Unfortunately, I also decided to get an abortion. I remember even two years earlier being so upset with a friend who told me she had gotten one. I believed that I would never under any circumstances ever abort a baby! What I didn't understand then was that we don't always know what we're capable of doing. God knows we are sinners, and what our weaknesses and breaking points are, even when we don't. I had already undergone so much loss, and my in-laws were threatening to sue me for custody of the baby, saying that their son would never pay child support.

They were very rich, and I had no money. I believed that they would make good on their threat, and I couldn't bear the thought of them raising my child and controlling all our lives. So I let my father-in-law, who had been strongly encouraging me to get one, pay for the abortion. I was far enough along that I had to go to a special clinic in downtown L.A. to get it. I never told anyone besides my sister, not even my mother until much later; everyone else I let think I had miscarried. I mourned the loss of that baby for a long time, and it became one more thing I had to let go of. No one talked to me about God and putting my life and trust in Him, or any of that. Neither the nurses at the clinic or the social worker that came to see me in my room talked about it as being a spiritual decision.

Putting it behind me, as I had done with so many other things, I continued to live a fairly normal life over the next four years, working at a small branch of the Bank of America on the Queen Mary, and trying to pay my bills, keep up friendships, and date. I rarely gave religion any thought. My sister and her husband moved away, and my mother finally settled down to married life with a wonderful man from Hungary. Things all around seemed settled until I got pregnant again in 1982. I went to church with my roommate and her family maybe two or three times while I was pregnant, but it made no impression on me. I only remember that it was a Protestant church, that I was bored, and completely uninterested in the services. This baby, however, I intended to keep, no matter how hard it might be. I named my newborn daughter Christie, having some vague idea in the far reaches of my mind that I wanted her to be connected to Christ, but I would drift further and further away before I would ever figure out what that meant. It would be quite some time before I would give my heart over, and I would have to take a very sinuous path to reach that point. I did not marry her father, though I had loved him. I also felt at the time that it would be too risky and too idealistic to count on anyone being around forever for us. He had been part of my healing, but now I had to grow up and find my own way. When Christie was four months old, my brother flew out from Atlanta in order to help me make the drive back to West Virginia, where I thought it would be easier for me to raise a child as a single parent. When we got settled in I became determined in my mind to never again be, or appear to be weak, needy, or too much in love. The thing is, God wants us to be the exact opposite!

———————————

25

In the fall of 1984 I started taking classes at a local community college. I had wanted to attend college after high school, but because of my family problems was never able to. Now, with a child, I wanted to go back and get a degree more than ever. And the up side of being so dirt poor was that I qualified for full financial aid! Grants would pay for my tuition, and loans would help me live. Fearing that I might never be able to complete a four-year program, I earned an Associates Degree in general education, taking all the courses I would need to transfer into a Bachelor Degree program if ever I could. I still did not trust my life. I had learned that a person's situation could always change on a dime, and I was taking nothing for granted. So, while I was there, I was soaking up an education like a dry sponge. I loved most of my classes: American history, literature, philosophy, psychology, and art history, though I was less crazy about economics, math, and science. And as seems to happen with many students, there was one professor in particular who influenced my thinking about life.

Dr. Jane Summerville taught American and women's literature. She was a very petite redheaded woman in her early fifties (I think), who wore long flowery skirts with blouses and vests, always seeming to be draped in layers of material; she wore hats, lots of jewelry, and lace-up granny boots and espadrilles. She was always talking about her travels and how she was going to retire to some island off the coast of mainland Greece and write. She wrote poetry, and engaged in a creative battle with another woman professor in some other state, publishing her poetry in magazines and journals. She lived alone in an old Victorian house in Marietta, Ohio, and even once took us to attend a Fiction Reading followed by a reception in the author's honor on a sternwheeler boat docked on the river. It was my first taste of what I considered to be a literary life, and this female professor of mine was actually living it right here! In the classroom she taught us nineteenth and twentieth century women's literature, and she was on fire with passion for the lives of those women, both the authors and their characters, explaining the literary movements that framed their works, and the themes that dominated their stories. She scribbled scores of notes onto the blackboard, and I copied them all down, hoping that I could commit them to memory, and more deeply understand what I felt was authenticating some of my own experiences and feelings of struggling as a woman in society. I was falling in love with literature, and she had been the conduit! The only problem was that this was one of the last courses I could take before earning my degree; however, I had found my passion, and I wanted to pursue it. This led me to investigate and then transfer to Marietta College, a small liberal arts college located about fifteen miles north from where I lived. Thankfully it all worked out. Though it was an extremely expensive private school, I received full financial aid for another two years! God was opening a door. A new course was set and I was on my way.

Passions for anything can be a powerful driving force, and whether we consciously follow them or not, they often dictate our lives. I believe that God gives them to us, and that He uses them to move us closer to Him, and to do his work. Satan also knows this and so tries to tempt us with negative outlets for our desires. But any desire that leads to God comes from him, and so while my mind was closed off to God, my heart was newly bursting open, albeit to literature. However, reading would be the chink in my armor that would lead me back to God, though it would take several more years. I had always loved to read from the time I first learned how, but had read mostly for entertainment, following my lust for crime solving and adventure in my earlier years, and then following my lust for romance throughout my early twenties. I can certainly attest to the fact that of the making of romance novels there is no end! Reading those things became like a drug to my soul, but one that could never satisfy. I swear, it seemed as though I yearned for nothing more than to be swept up off my feet, or even forcibly captured if necessary, by some domineering but gorgeous man who I would initially hate, but for whom I would eventually fall madly, passionately in love! Of course my own real life had none of that in it; in fact, it seemed to be almost hostile to any idea of love, real or otherwise. I had been losing any notion of what love was anyway, and was substituting lust in its place, even trying to convince myself that was better. Fortunately, while college would not immediately improve my tastes in men or how I interacted with them, college would definitely improve my tastes in reading.

I entered Marietta College, declaring a major in secondary education with an emphasis in English. But after two semesters of taking education courses, and after sitting in at local high schools, I knew I was on the wrong career path. My passion didn't seem to be for teaching; it was for literature. I felt like I was wasting time in my education classes, and taking valuable time away from being able to take the classes I really wanted, and so I switched majors. Of course I had plenty of people asking me what I was going to do with an English degree if I didn't plan on teaching. I couldn't answer them satisfactorily, but I felt intuitively that I had to listen to my own heart in this matter. So while at Marietta College I took thirty-six more hours in English on top of what I had taken at the community college. I studied film and literature; American literature, examining women in history and in fiction; Shakespeare' tragedies, comedies, and histories, and Chaucer's Canterbury Tales; I took a class in Introduction to Poetry, as well as a Victorian poetry class; I studied persuasive writing and self-expressive writing; and I studied literary criticism, which covered every language and writing theory from the time of the Greeks up through today. I took a few other courses in English, two theater classes, an anthropology class, two speech classes, two philosophy classes, and a host of other classes that also stretched me intellectually. I felt like I had been living in the dark and was entering the light! But the question still remained—what would I do after graduation?

It's important to pause here and discuss what I had been doing in my personal life while attending college. By the time I graduated, my daughter had finished first grade. For four years I had been dating various guys that I had either met from school or had met at the bars I started going out to on Friday nights with some girlfriends. While some guys I got emotionally tangled up with, others I did not. Most of the men I met at the bars had good jobs, and a couple even owned their own businesses; only two or three seemed likely to end up as losers. However, in regards to virtually every one of them, I felt that if I actually got married, I would end up bored to tears with my life. Meaning, every time I looked down the road at what my life would probably be like, I didn't like what I saw but only once. And when I announced to *him* that I might go to law school, he dropped me right away for a younger girl who had just started a career as an elementary school teacher. We had been dating about nine months. She had obviously been waiting in the wings. I never did date anyone who went to church. One time when Christie was still a baby I visited a Worldwide Church of God service in hopes of renewing some old friendships, but after the services were ended a group of three men escorted me into a very small room the size of a closet and started interrogating me about each member of my family. I felt very uncomfortable, and was almost reduced to tears. It also made me very mad, and so I determined never to see those people ever again. (However, a few years ago my sister and I were invited to attend a reunion given in our honor by some families with whom we had once been very close! And one other time, also a few years ago, my husband and I were invited by a splinter group to an overnight ox roast and square dance.) Other than that, when Christie was two I dated a guy whose parents went to church, and we went once with them on Christmas Eve. I also, one time, had an attraction for a guy who turned out to be a Christian, but who spent the evening telling me that I was going to hell if I didn't change my life and accept Christ. Of course that went over with me like a lead balloon! Several years later I ran into this same guy in a downtown bar. Noting that he was drunk, I couldn't help but ask him what had brought on this drastic change. (I had reminded him of the lecture he had once given me!) He told me that his father had died unexpectedly, and that he had lost all faith. Well, as far as I was concerned, that served him right! Not the death, but the loss of faith. Humph! Obviously it wasn't something that could get a person through tough times! It hadn't me, and it hadn't him either. The only other "spiritual" experience I had was when a girl from college told me about going to see this woman who read cards. She had even helped the local police out a couple of times when they reached a dead end in criminal cases. I made an appointment and went to see her. She read regular playing cards. Using two decks, she would lay them out on the kitchen table into a big pattern, reading them line-by-line, card-by-card, telling you your future. She told me I would eventually meet and marry a man, and then move several states away someplace close to a large body of water. We would not stay there, but would move again. She told me other things, but that's what I remember, mostly because that's what caught my interest. It did make me start thinking again about the spiritual world, which would raise questions that would send me off in a whole new direction! Also, I was getting ready to move to Oxford, Ohio, where I had decided to attend graduate school.

I was twenty-nine and Christie was six when we moved. I lost all the state assistance I had been receiving in West Virginia, and began living on student loans and the graduate assistantships I would earn by teaching. We found a small cottage-like house to live in, which was actually the parsonage that belonged to the Church of Christ sitting next door. Believe me when I say that the irony of that did not go unnoticed by me! "You'll never guess," I'd say before proceeding to tell my friends where we were living. The minister came over a couple of times to invite us to church, but I finally had to ask him quite adamantly to please leave us alone. He had been very kind and polite, but I wasn't ready yet for what he had to offer. But thankfully, God had no plans for leaving me alone. He was leading me even into a career. Though I had scored fairly well on the LSATs, the door had closed on my going to law school. Learning to view right and wrong through the lens of legal rhetoric would not be my path; nor would I enter the professional world of high finance. (I had been interviewed very seriously by a stock brokerage firm based in Pittsburgh who preferred graduates in the field of the humanities. Ironically they refused to hire me based on my personality profile! Ha!) Obviously God wanted me to continue studying in the field of English!

The study of literature is the study of human nature and the human condition. In other words, it seeks to establish some truth about the nature of humankind, to explore the relationships among people, and to explore the connection between people and society. While one does study the structure of the plot, the characters and their development, their external or internal conflicts and struggles, the setting, the methods of narration, irony, and symbolism, all of it is to get at theme. Theme is that core truth of what the author is actually saying *about* human nature or the human condition. After reading a story a reader tends to reflect on some aspect of life, using her own experiences, her knowledge, or her understanding before reaching a set of emotional and intellectual responses. (Granted, I have met people who are not reflective readers at all, but who want stories that only entertain or leave them with an immediate good feeling. However, they would not be students of literature.) Literature can further be studied through the lenses of culture and history, through psychology, or various philosophies such as Formalism, Marxism, or Feminism (and others too numerous to name here), which can each add a whole other layer to one's understanding. However, the more trained a student becomes in how to approach reading, that is, the more "academic" she becomes, the more closed off she is liable to be in regards to listening to her heart's first response, so much so that it eventually can become a strictly intellectual endeavor, or an endeavor to further a political agenda. This is what happens to most students in graduate school. Students, mimicking their professors and trying to get ahead in a very competitive atmosphere, often become pompous intellectuals, adopting a particular theory with the same kind of zealousness of the worst religious fanatic, arguing its value as if it contained the answers to all the problems of the world.

As an undergraduate I did not experience this tendency from my professors to adopt a theory and use it to "convert" students into a particular worldview. Instead, I was introduced primarily to the study of human nature, especially when I read the Greek tragedies, both the tragedies and comedies of Shakespeare, and the Canterbury Tales. When studying early American literature I read about the Puritans wanting religious freedom, but saw, through their stories, as well as other's stories, how many times their legalistic approach to religion, as well as their superstitious beliefs, had hurtful effects on different individuals and even on society as a whole. I studied the Age of Enlightenment, or the Age of Reason, which had been ushered in by scientific advancements and industrialization. I read story after story about how people turned to science or government to cure the problems of poverty, loneliness, ignorance, violence, or sickness and disease. This in turn resulted in the Romantic Movement, or a turning back to nature, and seeing God in nature as well as in one's self. In America, the Transcendentalists, who I liked, believed in both racial and gender equality at a time when others hadn't yet caught on. Henry David Thoreau's experimental living at Walden Pond, where he strived to live a life devoid of materialism, particularly inspired me. (This lead me to an interest in novels that explored utopian as well as distopian ideas.) I was also interested in Emerson's theory that the scope of the universe and man's position in it are fathomable not by the logic of human intellect, but by the divine spark of intuition. Like all transcendentalists, he glorified intuitive "reason" over more rational, experiential understanding. Maybe this appealed to me because I had spent my youth being taught an intellectual approach to God, albeit one that was many times devoid of logic! He also believed in being self-reliant, a concept that also greatly appealed to me. Both Thoreau and Emerson's essays offered up new ideas about religion and God that I had never considered.

However, having to read on, I learned that within a very short time the Victorians would face a loss of Faith unlike any that societies had encountered before them. Darwin published his *Origin of Species* in 1859, introducing a theory of evolution that would completely shatter any romantic notion about nature. I saw the results of this in the literature written after that period when authors portrayed life as it really was for the lower and middle classes, struggling to survive in a world now deemed very hostile, and without God. The Romantics' idealism, along with their rejection of reason, died out, as life in the early twentieth century brought a world war, followed by new wealth and prosperity, followed by economic disaster. Literature of those periods reflected lives lived in excess, as well as lives lived in impoverishment. While I read stories about people who had dreams and tried to follow them, most of the people saw their dreams destroyed either because of a condition in nature beyond their control, or else because of misplaced trust in man, or poor judgment of man's nature. Most literature seemed completely depressing. Happy endings seemed like they were over. Then the world experienced a second war, and we saw a holocaust and evil dictators on both sides of the political spectrum fighting for world domination. We faced total annihilation. In literature, happy endings *were* over. Life became meaningless, and the story itself lost its ability to evoke meaning or instruct any more; its new purpose became solely about experimentation of form and of subject. Characters would begin the struggle to find meaning in anything and everything. (Pulp fiction, of course, written strictly to entertain, was still keeping the appetites of the masses satiated.)

So why did I want to keep studying all this? In part, I think because I was still searching for answers. I felt many of the same personal and spiritual struggles that appeared as themes in so much of the literature. Reading it actually became a spiritual endeavor for me! What I was seeing through literature was that all people, no matter when they lived, how rich or how poor they were, what class, race, nationality, creed, or gender defined them, they all loved and suffered because they were human! And as much as I wanted to throw out Christianity because it seemed to me to be more of the problem than the answer, I wanted as vehemently to throw out God as I had witnessed being done in the latter half of the twentieth century! I also was struggling with accepting that God could exist and let all this suffering happen. But one thing I couldn't accept was the belief that man was like the animals; unlike animals, man had something maybe like a soul. Man had the ability to reflect and dream, to interpret even the most abstract of concepts, to create, to manipulate and lie, and to even idealize and worship. I knew we didn't develop these attributes just as survival instincts, and therefore, as much as I wanted to, I was not able to throw out the idea of God. While my professors loved that I was not Christian, they preferred students who were atheists. However, they weren't too terribly concerned that I would misguide my own students, because all I was at that point, at best, was a Deist. I was, though, compromising with them by my willingness to adopt the rhetoric of more leftist politics. However, I wasn't a very passive student in regards to just letting them fill me up like an empty vessel. I had already learned earlier in my life that people can be wrong in their beliefs, and so I wanted to figure out the answers to life's questions on my own. This stubborn streak of mine was not popular among my literature professors. One even accused me of not being truly "academic." This in part is why I switched from studying literature to studying Composition & Rhetoric. While I was in graduate school I would continue to read critical literary theory, but I would add to it the study of rhetorical theory, which included the study of the origin and meaning of language systems and symbols, as well as how the written word is constructed.

I would eventually be particularly drawn to the theories put forth by Carl Jung concerning archetypes, which would lead me to reading Joseph Campbell, and studying the hero's journey. I had already come to love the greatest mythic hero's journey ever written in my opinion,

J. R. R. Tolkien's *The Lord of the Rings*. I had read it back in high school about three times, and became a collector of all Tolkien's works. Like with *The Lord of the Rings*, all archetypal stories, that is, all mythologies, fairytales, and hero's journeys contain archetypes that exist as part of a collective unconscious, which include as part of it symbols of Birth (or the Fool), Initiation, Withdrawal, Quest, Entering the Realms of Death, and Confrontation with the Devil. Good and Evil in these types of stories are always clearly discernable. However, in other types of literature, as in life, the delineation between good and evil become skewed, and thus it's more difficult to have a hero. A hero, though, after entering the realms of death and confronting evil, is able to be reborn and becomes transformed. Frodo Baggins is an example of a hero. While I was interested in all the archetypes, this confrontation with the devil, or the trickster, got more of my attention.

All literature, it seemed to me, eventually leads readers to a place where, if they are reflective, must face the question as to what they believe to be the nature of good and evil, and whether they believe mankind is ultimately good or evil. If one accepts that mankind is primarily good, then a person could place her faith in man's ability to ultimately bring about universal good, though there has yet to be much evidence for this happening. Or, if one accepts instead, that man is primarily evil, then she has either to decide that there is no point to being good, or else choose to settle for trying to make one little piece of the world (or, if she is more idealistic, the larger world as much as she can affect it), as good as she can while she lives. Whichever side a person comes down on though, in regards to man, it still leaves open the larger question of the nature of good and evil, which leaves open the question of the existence of God! Since I personally could not accept that mankind evolved, though part of me would have preferred that he had, I was left with a big problem. It seemed evident to me that evil existed, that man more than not perpetuated evil, and that he was unable to do good consistently long enough to counteract the evil that existed. I could not accept that man could fix man's problem. Therefore, I wanted to examine whether there could be an idea of God that I could accept as making any sense. I was not, however, interested in a form of spirituality that would be an escape! (And concerning one's reading habits—I would argue that fiction written for the sole purpose of entertaining the reader, or fiction that allows a reader to escape, cannot be affectively spiritual, and could even stunt one's spiritual growth.)

In grad school most of my professors claimed to have the whole matter settled. They did not believe in God, and they believed that human

The author at Tolkien's grave, located outside Oxford, England.

kind was primarily good. Half of my professors stood in the Marxist camp, arguing that all the ills of the world were because of the excessive amount of wealth that had been amassed by a few, namely Capitalists, and that if we could stamp out capitalism eventually all would be well. Other of my professors (mostly female) argued that all the ills of the world stemmed primarily from the patriarchal domination practiced by most civilizations and institutions. Either way, they both seemed to agree that power was the issue. There was only so much of it to go around, and that one group, either the economically disadvantaged, or women and any other racial or gendered minority, had to take it from their oppressors. Both liked the term "revolution." I was listening to them all and taking notes! However, what really seemed to have my interest, so much so that's it's a wonder I ever got any work done, was this issue of God. It was close coming up on a decade when I last entertained the idea that if there were a God then there had to be an absolute truth. I had decided then to put that whole question on the shelf, and so God became for me a moot point, until God reappeared framed within academic discourse. In college God was significant only in reference to something historical or cultural, or in reference to absolute ignorance by the uneducated. The Bible became just another piece of literature. In its place came great thinkers and doers with new political and philosophical ideologies written down in other great texts. But as I pointed out, it hadn't been quite settled for me. Now keep in mind that based on my past there was no way that I would be drawn to Christianity, whether it took the form of fundamentalism, evangelicalism, or liberalism. I had no background that would enable me to differentiate between any form of Protestantism, and I was no longer interested in Catholic theology. It was basically all the same to me, and I wanted to prove all of it wrong! What further fueled my dislike for Christianity besides the fact that most academics scoffed at it, was what I was hearing about television evangelists, who were committing adultery, or embezzling large sums of money, or building large empires, all the while condemning the rest of the world! Their lives seemed as self-absorbed or corrupt as any! I had also been noting, at the same time, incongruencies in the lives of some of my professors in terms of the ideologies they "professed" versus how they lived, which made Peyton Place seem boring! In any case, I would hold in reservation and question anything anybody tried to convert me to until I could prove its worth.

There was one idea in particular that I completely began to reject and despise, but was basic to Christianity. It was the notion that everybody had only one chance to be saved. You either got it right before you died, or else. I had already come to a place where I understood that most people had a lot of suffering in their lives. I would never believe in a God who only gave people one chance! Even I, as imperfect as I was, felt enough compassion for the human race to do better than that! Consequently, I became very interested in investigating any belief system that allowed for the idea that people reincarnated. With this as my first goal, I looked towards the East. What I really wanted was to model my search for truth based on a novel I had loved as an undergrad, entitled *Siddhartha*. Written by Hermann Hesse, it is the story of a soul's quest for the meaning of man's existence on earth. The young boy Siddhartha, born into the religious upper class, meets the Buddha, but cannot be content with a disciple's role. He must confront and experience all that life has to offer, religious and secular, all the while working out his own destiny. I, like Siddhartha wanted to become a spiritual explorer, investigating for my own self what was truth and what was empty lies. I would have to do this, and be a student and a mother all at the same time.

I would start with Buddhism. Wanting to be an exemplary student in whatever I undertook to study, I checked out of the library every book I could find on the subject. I remember carrying a stack of books on Buddhism with me into French class around the second or third day of classes. There was one guy in there that took particular note of what I was reading and made some flippant joke about it. Five or six weeks into that first semester I ended up dropping French and later took Spanish, but we would remain friends. He would later become my husband, but that would be several years down the road. Also, unbeknownst to me then, he would play a role in my conversion. He was Christian. In the meantime I would be working on becoming a good Buddhist.

The premise of Buddhism is first, the omnipresence of suffering (a truth I had already accepted from reading so much literature), and secondly, that the cause of most of our suffering is desire, the desire of self for selfish gratification (I also believed this to be true, having likewise verified it from all the literature I'd read). Thirdly, that which has been caused can be removed by the removal of the cause, and finally, by following the Eightfold Path, one can remove the cause of the suffering, the self and its desires, and thus put an end to suffering. Following the Eightfold Path is a moral philosophy that includes having a correct mental attitude, right motive, right speech, right action, right livelihood, right effort, right meditation, and right discipline. It is important on this path to break the cycle of suffering and desire, and to thus be free from Karma, which is the Law of Cause and Effect. The goal of any seeker is to be free from suffering, meaning each person must die to the will of the Self, which is the ego. For Siddhartha that Self had been arrogance and intellectualism. One has to die to oneself in order to live in a state of Nirvana, which is a release from the limitations of a separate existence. Intuitive Knowledge gained on the Path is believed to be pure, and it is only our evaluation or interpretation that labels it good or bad, right or wrong when trying to translate it into a concept. In other words, these are merely concepts wrapped up in the Ego, and are not real. This, I wanted to investigate!

Anyway, the Path is eventually supposed to lead to unity with the One that lacks any definition other than Universal Consciousness. You can see that this idea of good and evil and universal consciousness played a role in my gravitating towards Jungian theory. The One, to be certain, was not God; it was not a Being. While Buddhism has become increasingly popular in the U.S. (Richard Geer is perhaps the most famous American practitioner), it's Eightfold Path is extremely difficult to live and work out, and therefore Seekers often turn to a more watered down form of spirituality; Buddhism mixed with Transcendentalism, Hinduism, Native American spiritualism, and Celtic and occult worship, has fallen under the label of "New Age." This is where I ended up myself once I questioned the premise that all desire led to suffering. Some desires, as far as I could discern, seemed to be good, and just, and some even almost necessary! I even thought that sometimes suffering led to the desire for change, which could be good, and that some suffering might even be noble if done for another human being! Therefore, not being able to fully accept the premises, I realized that if I took this seriously, according to Buddhism, I could never be released from the Karmic wheel. It would take an eternity to pay off Karmic debts! And that meant that I could never stop reincarnating! I definitely wanted to be able to live more than one life, but the idea of it's being a penalty did not appeal to me. I believed that most everyone's life contained suffering, and oftentimes in extreme measures, but according to the Buddhist Law of Karma, people brought their suffering on themselves, thus the wheel was turned by man's own hand. I wanted to be able to return to the earthly plane when and how I wanted. I still believed that mankind suffered, but maybe we chose it for some spiritual reason, rather than to pay off a debt. I also found it difficult to be enthusiastic about a universal collective consciousness, when I was part of a culture that encouraged individuality and uniqueness.

Thankfully, the New Age movement offered up a veritable smorgasbord of beliefs to keep me searching in books written on every subject from the law of karma (which has a few variations to it, depending on the belief system); to reincarnation; to astrology; to chakras; to animal wisdom and medicine; to shamanism; to wise women, witches and goddesses; to Taoism, and Zen Buddhism. While studying each of these took up much of my time, what ultimately got my interest was Tarot. The Tarot grew out of a card game popular in Europe in the fourteenth century, probably carried back from the Middle East by the Crusaders. Gypsies coming to the West at this time adopted them for fortune telling. Each deck of cards is based on a particular mythology or culture, so they may be Pagan (i.e. based on Greek mythology), Celtic, Norse, Native American, Hindu, Tibetan, Mayan, African, Egyptian, or they may be based on a subject such as the Arthurian legend, Jungian theory, the women's movement, or even be based on the works of a particular artist such as Salvador Dali. There is even a deck based on the *Lord of the Rings*! Each suit of cards in the Minor Arcana (which deal with life's run-of-mill events) is based on the elements of earth (the pentacle), fire (the sword), water (the cup), and air (the wand), which would signify material achievement; mental or spiritual struggle, or conflict; relationships, romance, or creativity; and adventure or pursuit of a vision, respectively. Each suit, of course, would start with the Ace, move through the numbers one through nine, and include the page, the knight, the queen, and the king. The Major Arcana contains twenty-two cards that are allegorical, or archetypal. They illustrate life principles and the journey of the soul from birth to enlightenment. Modern readings of tarot tend to focus less on prediction and more on psychological understanding. They attempt to explore the subconscious and connect people's inner and outer experiences. Learning to read the symbols not only aids in developing intuition, but also becomes a tool for reflection and meditation. Is it any wonder that I became interested in these card decks? I literally began to read books on the mythologies and cultures themselves, trying to grasp the wisdom and truth of each one! Actually, I was studying religions of the world! And I was discovering that they had many of the same elements, or archetypes contained within their stories. It's a wonder I could get my graduate studies done, but it's no wonder I couldn't give myself over to the "intellectualism" required by the academy. It couldn't feed my soul! I did love the reading, and the in-depth discussions we would have in and out of class, and I still find these types of discussions to be exhilarating!

Another thing I especially loved was that the English department would bring in professionals to speak from the fields of literature and rhetoric. I got to hear Peter Elbow, a prolific writer in the field of Composition, speak; and I had the opportunity to become good friends with bell hooks, who has written a dozen books, and who at the time taught at Oberlin College in Ohio. When she got bored, herself, with all the intellectual discussions and schmoozing and hobnobbing going on around her she would turn to me for a more spiritual connection. She would call me every time she came to Oxford, much to the dismay of the professors who would invite her. Many times we read Mother Earth Tarot cards together and talked on the phone about boyfriends. My daughter, Christie, and I even spent a weekend at her home once. Besides her, the English department also brought in well-known popular authors like Margaret Atwood. There was nothing so fun as attending wine and cheese receptions after hearing an author read, and then discuss his or her work! I guess if that could have been it, I could have been satisfied for a long time. But in the end a person must stand alone in front of a mirror and face herself! Myth and story had become my mirror. And I couldn't just approach it from an intellectual point of view. I wanted to see the whole person down to the core.

My daughter, in the meantime, became best friends with a girl from a Pentecostal background. Her family, who developed and managed property in Oxford, basically adopted Christie as their own. They took her with them everywhere, including church on Wednesday nights. They were so incredibly kind and generous to her, as they were to me. Even though they knew I was not Christian, they never tried to convert me. What they did do was set one example for me of a family with Christian values who could offer their love and support, and undoubtedly their prayers, and let God do the rest. I never argued against their beliefs to Christie except for one time, when after attending church camp for a week together, her friend

The author and bell hooks at Miami University, 1990

told Christie that since she did not speak in tongues she was not saved. I had to explain to Christie that I believed this was not true. Anyway, she seemed to be enjoying the social aspects of it all so much, and I felt I could counterbalance any Christian theology she might be getting with a New Age spiritual perspective. Hence, I taught my daughter everything I learned. One time I took her with me to a Native American/ Goddess-type spiritual gathering, which met on the night of a full moon. Outside, we welcomed in the spirits from the four directions, and then went inside, and sat in a circle cleansed by sage, surrounding lit candles. Passing around a talking stick, each of the about a dozen women had the opportunity to speak, saying whatever was on her mind in terms of blessings, prayers, or concerns. It was all quite matriarchal and spiritual. When we were finished, we invited the spirits to dismiss us, and to put out the candles. Christie started blowing out the candle nearest her, when the woman who was leading us hastily reprimanded her for doing so. I asked her how

Christie could possibly know that it required fanning out the flame instead of blowing it out. For that woman it was a rule that could not be broken, even by an innocent child! And I had another errant and rigid belief to unteach my daughter.

Since I was into New Age spiritualism to find truth, and not to escape, I would find myself moving through it, leaving different groups, and discarding different beliefs as I found them to be empty. I was, however, collecting bits and pieces of truth, or insight. I was also becoming intensely aware of the existence of evil. Even when reading Tarot I sensed to stay away from certain decks that were designed to lead a reader into the psychology of evil. I wouldn't go near a Ouija Board, nor would I participate in séances. There were some people involved in the occult that were primarily interested in practicing evil, and you could feel it emanating from them. Even among practitioners of Wicca there were those who turned towards healing and those who turned towards black magic. Evil in the occult definitely seems to be about power, control, and manipulation, and can be absolutely frightening! It would be impossible to convince me that evil does not exist in the world. But whenever people lose a belief in its existence in one form, it will take on another. Satan is the ultimate Trickster and liar.

On a brighter note, I was also developing my intuitive, or feminine spiritual side. I immersed myself in the study of the divine as feminine. But in whatever endeavor I met other seekers, one thing I was discovering was that everyone had the same basic reason for searching: they were driven by a desire to satisfy a longing in their souls for meaning. Most of the seekers I met were extremely educated, and most had experienced Christianity as being too narrow and patriarchal, and its followers as often being too judgmental and/or hypocritical. Organized religion had begun to feel like living under the law. For the Jews, the law under the old covenant had been a yardstick to show them how difficult it was to obey and keep all of the rules. Just read Leviticus if you want a reminder of the full extent of it. I had myself experienced something like it growing up. The Pharisees, though, prided themselves on building an even bigger hedge around it so that they could brag that they were obeying it, and then some! That is one story of human nature, and we see it in action in Christians who have put hedges around Christ's message, taking the heart right out of it. If one can avoid not only sinful action, but also sinful word and thought, then one is a better Christian! It sounds very much like the Buddhist Eightfold Path! I think Christ was making the point that we can never do it, that is, we can never be good enough to save ourselves. Try living under the law of karma if this isn't clear! It is a new covenant yardstick used to measure one's righteousness. Even though we know that no one is righteous, but is made that way only by the Grace of Christ, we still feel we need measurable proof for comparison purposes. This new form of legalism even spills over into what some Christians believe they can read. For example, I have been told many times by many Christian students that they could not read such and such a book because it contained characters who sinned! Granted, reading fiction written for escape and entertainment could very well lead one down a sinful path, but reading literature that requires some engagement with the mind will very doubtfully lead anywhere but to critical self-examination. It could even open one's mind enough to let some love for the suffering condition of mankind break a person's heart! Good literature goes deeper than reflecting society's ills, it critiques them as well. Many of the people I met over the years who were seeking answers among New Age spiritualism had experienced some form of suffering or pain in their lives. Many have lived extremely imperfect or sin filled lives. They are looking to heal and possibly save themselves. This form of spiritualism seems to offer that possibility. Its key element is karma, a law of harmony, or perfect relationship between all things everywhere. Its lesson is that when we can learn to see everything in the light of love, our every act will reflect the harmony of the divine! To this end, we choose to reincarnate upon this earth until we learn this lesson of love. It sounds beautiful and inviting and open to all, without condemnation. There is no need for a savior. Everyone will eventually save himself, and time is man's friend.

This definitely attracted me, except for one problem. While people who profess this basic belief acknowledge that there are bad people in the world, they do not seem to have an ultimate conclusion to the problem of evil. Still I was driven to find the answer to that question. What happens to the people who don't learn to love, but choose the opposite path? It seems that evil exists within people; are they building up such bad karma that they will continue to come back as more and more evil? Do evil souls exist in the spirit world alongside souls of good people, which if they do means that we will never be able to escape evil, even in the spirit realm? Do they have eternity to work out their karma, or will there be a limit to how much evil a person is allowed to build up? It was going to take a lot of faith if I were going to accept that all souls, no matter how bad a path they were heading down, would just eventually *choose* of their own free will to become good. Or, what if evil really is just a concept that only exists on this plane of existence so that we can learn spiritual lessons. But if evil doesn't exist anywhere but here, and souls keep reincarnating, what is the point? Can spirits not learn and grow in a perfect environment? Or, might evil exist just for fun, or in order to entertain souls on earth? This seemed unlikely. These were questions I couldn't get anybody to answer. Almost everyone responded in the exact same way: "There's too much to think about, and I'll just wait until I die or until my next life to figure it out." The end. And I might have left it there too if it weren't for this suffering issue! What terrible thing might I have to suffer in my next life? Could I do anything to prevent it in this one? And shouldn't I at least try to figure it all out? I even worried about my general dislike for Christians. Really though, I think I actually only knew two or three. But what if I had to learn to love all of them in principle, which could mean that I might have to come back as one if I didn't learn that lesson in this life! Ugh! Most people just shrug all this off with an "I'll worry about it later" attitude. Why couldn't I?

My theory is that as long as our minds are asking questions, God can lead us through anything to find Him. This is what He did for me. Remember that guy I mentioned earlier from French class, the one who was Christian? Well, we had an unexplainable attraction for one another, and so dated off and on for four years. Whenever I would ask him any kind of theological or philosophical question, he would always give me a Bible based response, never compromising, but never preaching at me or putting me down either. One day when I must have seemed more open to suggestion than normal, he mentioned that since I was such a huge Tolkien fan I might like to read some fiction by C. S. Lewis, who had been one of the Inklings, the literary group of which Tolkien was also member, and with whom he had also been friends.

He lent me his copies of *The Screwtape Letters* and *The Great Divorce*. When I finished reading them I was wowed! I always read with my truth detectors on, and what I recognized as truth in *The Screwtape Letters* was how evil, in the form of Wormwood, works on destroying the very soul of man, taking every chance and opportunity in every aspect of man's life to lead him further away from knowing God. His uncle Screwtape has been a student of human nature for thousands of years, analyzing man's every word and action, so as to better enable him to predict man's egoistic driven decision making. He himself wanted to be God, and he understands that we do too. Having been a fallen angel, Satan is the opposite of Michael, not of God. And his nature, as with all the demons that chose to follow him, is depraved, and that as a result of his own free will. Man has this same free will to choose to either humble himself to love, or to listen to his selfish ambition and greed. Satan is not out to scare us; he is out to trick us! Not that he doesn't enjoy giving us a good fright whenever he can. But really, that kind of thing usually just sends someone running in the opposite direction, and thus defeats his purpose. He will, however, whisper in our ears every deceitful lie he can get us to believe about our selves, others, and God.

The author in front of the Eagle and the Child pub in Oxford, England, the famous meeting place of the Inklings, which included Tolkien and Lewis.

What I recognized as truth in *The Great Divorce* again had to do with human nature, and man's will, if it is strong enough, to hang onto whatever our egos need, thus creating our own hells. The fact that our egos separate us from each other and from love is not enough to make us let go of whatever it is we choose to cling to. For some the will is too strong to say to God, *Thy* Will be done. He will not throw us into hell; we will put ourselves there! Isn't that what the law of karma teaches too? In this way our selfish desires for gratification become our suffering, but we must willingly let them go. Anything we put before our love for God becomes our god, and controls us. Oh, wow! Who was this C. S. Lewis? I had to read more, so I picked up his autobiographical work, *Surprised by Joy*. I read about his life, and his interest in mythology, and how Tolkien said to him that Christianity was a myth that just happened to be true. That is wasn't simply about finding the one true religion among thousands of religions that were false, the question was "Where had religion reached its true maturity?" Lewis said it had to be in Hinduism or in Christianity. But, ultimately if ever a myth had become fact, had become incarnated, it was in Christianity. The Word became flesh; God became man. The final step for me in accepting Christianity was to understand why. God was closing in on me, and I had to make a decision. It made sense that a Creator would love His creation (just ask any writer, artist, or parent), and He loved us! But, in His love He gave us free will, so that we could choose to love Him in return; but we, like Lucifer, turned against Him in order to satisfy our own desires, which have caused us a great amount of suffering and pain. He hears our cries. Because we can never save ourselves we need a Savior. God came down to save us. And while we recognize that laying down one's life to save another is the highest form of love one man can do for another, we still can't accept this gift from God. I, however, had *finally* come to understand that I needed a Savior! That I wanted one seemed a miracle. There was no other story, no other myth that contained such a possibility. Whoever said that the story of God coming to earth was The Greatest Story Ever Told, had not understated it! And the rest of the story is that evil and pain and suffering will end. It will not go on. There will be no more tears! Only Christ had this kind of plan. By the time I finished reading *Surprised by Joy*, I was beginning to be a Christian, and by the time I finished reading Lewis' apologetic work, *Mere Christianity*, I was converted!

If all things come from God, then all things can lead us back to Him, and will, if our hearts stay open. I had seen glimpses of God as He had made

Himself known through other religions and mythologies. As C. S. Lewis put it, "God has sent down pictures of himself so that we might desire Him." We can find pictures of him in nature, as the Native Americans and then the Transcendentalists both believed, though it's not the complete picture. The Greeks and the Romans' pagan religion gave them a glimpse of God. Paul knew about their religion when he stood in Athens at the meeting of the Areopagus (Acts 17:22–23) and mentioned the altar they had built to an unknown god. Wanting to gain a hearing, he complimented them on the fact that they were very religious. Then he explained the Good News of Christ. He offered a completion to their story. Here's the picture they had: They already understood the love of a god or goddess for a man or woman, thus their desire to have intercourse with them; they knew that man could become half god; they knew that man must obey the gods; they knew that sometimes during religious festivals the gods would require sacrifices for appeasement; they knew there was a god to rule over every aspect of life, and who controlled it; they knew that the gods were constantly watching them and interacting with them, and heard their prayers (Jupiter would actually hold his earphone down); they knew that the gods usually demanded absolute adoration and worship; they knew the gods were both creators of life and destroyers of it; they knew there was an underworld where evil existed; they knew the gods loved beauty; they knew the gods would often show mercy and forgiveness; they knew the gods would test people's motives, that they could see beyond the outward appearance; they knew the gods understood man's weaknesses towards wealth and beauty (they understood human nature); and finally, at their worst the gods were annoying and a little better than men. They were ready for a God who was perfect, and who could transform their lives. Throughout the history of the universe, man has had the desire to know why we are here, where everything came from, and what happens after death. Every culture has created stories to answer these questions, but the unbelievable thing is that every culture has created the same archetypes. That is, the big picture hasn't changed, only the details. The archetypes lead us to God. Christ didn't just come to fulfill the Law, but to save all of mankind. The universe had his name all over it, and had been waiting! Of all the stories I read throughout human history, detailing man's nature and man's suffering, and his desire to make a god out of something, anything, this One myth "that just happened to be true" was it. Lewis knew it when he sat down to write *The Chronicles of Narnia*, and Tolkien knew it when he wrote *The Lord of the Rings*. Evil must be destroyed in the end, and the most unlikely heroes are the ones who start out as fools. That had been me.

The author sitting in the study of C. S. Lewis at his home,
the Kilns, in Oxford, England.

The author standing at the grave of C. S. Lewis, located outside of Oxford, England.

4

Favorite Books from My Personal Library

ONCE I became a Christian, I wanted to go back and revisit books that I had previously read that had Christian themes and elements. I also needed to do this because I began teaching at a very conservative Christian college that fought the idea that their students should read anything but works of a "Christian nature." However, I quickly became interested in broadening the definition of what constituted Christian literature, and so began researching into its possible perimeters, as I had up to that point never given any thought to that particular way of categorizing literature. However, being both a student and a professor of literature, I wasn't satisfied with limiting my own reading. To the contrary, I wanted to continue to explore the variety of literary genres and themes, as well as literature that would cross boundaries of religion, as I had done before converting to Christianity. Also, as I began to travel extensively throughout Europe and the Middle East, I became interested in literature written by authors from around the globe, as well as in spiritual travel writing. Eventually I would come to use these works in my classes when I taught at other colleges, both Christian and secular. And as only God could have foreseen, since I earned my degree, I have taught classes in American literature, ancient, modern, and contemporary world literature, literature of the Middle East, and Christian literature. I have also taught introductory classes in creative writing, including poetry, fiction, and creative non-fiction; and I have taught the spiritual memoir, gender and writing, and women's literature and writing courses. While having added books to support these courses into my own personal library, it has become clear with one glance that God has definitely used the passion he gave me for reading, and then taken it beyond my dreams!

The following list of works is meant to be in addition to the works for which I included reader's guides. I would also like to add that there are a great many outstanding literary works that do not contain anything overtly Christian, or have any Christian symbols or metaphors or any single element that could be labeled Christian. While the list is overwhelmingly lengthy, I am including here only a short list of my favorites. Likewise, I am not including every Christian title because, again, that list would also be too long. What I do include are titles that I think should not be overlooked when planning a book club syllabus, or when planning your own personal library because they would most certainly add both literary depth and breadth. And while this is a partial listing of fictional titles, I have also included some that are non-fiction, primarily diaries, memoirs, and spiritual travel writing because they read very much like fiction and contain the same high literary merit as do the works of fiction. I also include works from contemporary Christian mystics, as I have found myself especially drawn to them, maybe because my own journey has offered me a look into the realm of the spirit, where I have so desperately sought to know God. What I leave out are spiritual works that are overtly non-Christian, such as the Sufi mystic poets, or one of my favorite Arab writer's, Kahlil Gibran, all Native American writers, and many, many others who I would strongly recommend, and who offered me over the years profound glimpses of God.

Finally, I have included works of fiction from notable and award-winning authors from around the world who try to shed light on the oppression felt by people who live under political regimes not sympathetic to the development of the human spirit. It is my belief that as we learn to love God, and then learn to love and take care of our selves, that we will become more interested in opening our hearts up to the rest of humanity. I think it is very important that we realize from a position of love that the world is in desperate need of a Savior. The works I listed may be painful to read, but I think necessary in terms of making us see the world the way God sees it. We must be willing to have our hearts broken. But love for others must never be just an abstract ideal, which is what I believe it is when we declare a "love the sinner but hate the sin" mentality. If we cannot even read about people whose lives have been devastated by living in a sinful world, and who may or may not understand that they need a way out, then how will we ever put our love into real action? This is what I believe a deeper spirituality calls for.

World Classics

The Epic of Gilgamesh

This Sumerian Epic is the oldest known story in the world; preserved on clay tablets found in Mesopotamia, it parallels the Old Testament in terms of the fall of man and death to mankind, and with its Flood story that agrees with many of the details in the Genesis story of Noah.

Geoffrey Chaucer, *The Canterbury Tales*

An unfinished collection of twenty-four stories narrated by each pilgrim in a traveling group going from Southwark, England to Canterbury in order to help pass the time more pleasantly. During the time of Chaucer the English were still deeply religious and thoroughly Catholic in their doctrines and practices, but what distinguishes these tales are their humanistic and fallible qualities. The pilgrimage brought together in an unlikely group a cross-section of English society, from the nobility and clergy, to the commoner, and thus their stories are a mixture of the secular and the religious, the worldly and the spiritual.

Dante [Alighieri], *The Divine Comedy*

A medieval poem, or allegorical work, consisting of three parts, each part an expression of one person in the Trinity: *Inferno*, the power of the Father, *Purgatorio*, the wisdom of the Son, and *Paradiso*, the love of the Holy Spirit. Each section looks at the state of man's soul not only after death but in life as well, as he discovers the life of faith in a faithless world.

John Bunyan, *The Pilgrim's Progress*

A seventeenth-century tale of Christian, Mr. Worldly Wiseman, Giant Despair, Hopeful, and Ignorance who are on an emotional and spiritual journey, spiced with Bunyan's satirical perceptions of the vanity and hypocrisy of his own society.

John Milton, *Paradise Lost*

A seventeenth-century epic poem of Satan's banishment from Heaven, the ensuing war between Heaven and Hell, and Satan's continuing struggle for revenge that leads to the Garden of Eden, the temptation and fall of Adam and Eve, and mankind's final redemption.

James Joyce, *A Portrait of the Artist as a Young Man*

This is the story about Stephen Dedalus, a sensitive and creative youth who rebels against his family, and his religious education from Jesuit priests, deciding not to become a priest himself, instead committing himself to the artistic life. He spends the entire story struggling with the theology of Roman Catholicism, and the rhapsody of teenage love.

James Joyce, *Dubliners*

This collective novel is written in fifteen stories, each one exemplifying the spiritual poverty and moral bankruptcy afflicting Joyce's contemporaries. However, Joyce believes in the possibility of redemption, thus in the collection's finale, "The Dead," the character Gabriel Conroy, a university graduate and teacher, is allowed a new vision of human limitation to which he responds with compassion, and is allowed a profound epiphany.

Georges Bernanos, *The Diary of a Country Priest*

This is the story of the life of a young French country priest who not only understands his people and portrays them with insight, but reveals his own joys and sorrows.

Graham Greene, *The Power and the Glory*

Set in crooked, anticlerical 1930's Mexico, and carrying in it the theme of "blessed are the poor in spirit," it is the story of a priest on the run, who while being hunted down tries to keep performing his priestly duties moved by his compassion for humanity and battling with his own sinful human behavior. A modern crucifixion story, which ends inevitably in the Church's triumph.

Graham Greene, *The Heart of the Matter*

The main character, Scobie, is a police official in a small coastal African town during the early years of WWII. Though he is basically a decent person, and a converted Catholic, he can no longer satisfy or tolerate his wife's concerns with appearances and the way the socialites in town regard her. Trying to separate himself from his wife, Scobie strikes up a tenuous relationship with Yusef, a suspected Syrian smuggler. Scobie also falls for Helen, a young widow, who only serves to intensify his unhappiness, and thus he must try to reconcile his dead love for his wife with his affections for Helen, his career, and his relationship to Yusef, all within the context of his Catholic faith. In the end, believing that he has let everybody down, including himself and God, Scobie comes to feel that his own death is the only thing that can accomplish happiness for those he loves. The theme, as expressed in this work, is that human relationships are implicitly inferior to the relationship that we may choose to experience with the divine.

Franz Kafka, *The Trial*

Joseph K., an ordinary man, wakes up one day to find that he has been accused of a crime he did not commit, a crime whose nature is never revealed to him. Once arrested, he is released, but must report to court on a regular basis—an event that proves maddening, as nothing is ever resolved. As he grows more uncertain of his fate, his personal life becomes increasingly unpredictable. He is not only unable to determine what he has done; he is also unable to know what to do about it. As K. tries to gain control, he succeeds only in accelerating his own excruciating downward spiral. Kafka writes in such a way as to leave the reader frustrated, an ordeal that in the end provides a glimpse into what his protagonist was enduring. The theme is moral justice, and Joseph K. is a metaphor for man who, though he may not have committed any specific act of sin, is yet in the state of sinfulness. In other words, he is under the curse of the fall. As Kafka once wrote, "The state that we find ourselves is sinful, quite independent of guilt." But sadly, for Joseph K., there is no grace.

Alan Paton, *Cry, The Beloved Country*

This story about South Africa, a black man's country under a white man's law, is set against the background of a land and people torn apart by racial injustice, in what was supposed to be a Christian nation. Book One of the story opens with a cry against injustice in South Africa as the old Zulu pastor, Stephen Kumalo, journeys from his remote tribal village to search in several black townships for his son who has vanished, and whom he later finds out has killed the son of a powerful white man known as a friend to the blacks. However, in Book Two a yearning for justice pervades as the spirit of Abraham Lincoln's ghost haunts the study of a murdered man, whose father, in subsequent actions, is motivated by Lincoln's words. Finally, love becomes the answer in this novel, though it is a tough love that not only pulls a person through pain, but that unites people who have every reason to be enemies, and thus it is a love that forgives.

Elie Wiesel, *Night*

Part of a trilogy that can stand on its own, this short novel is a close autobiographical account of events that transpired in Wiesel's own life as he made the long journey to Birkenau, Auschwitz, and Buchenwald, all the while wondering where God was in the midst of such horrors as he experienced. But he found no answers. He lost his family, his innocence, and eventually his God While the story is short, it very powerfully portrays the misery, suffering, and brutality, as well as the sadness and desolation that Weisel survived.

J. R. R. Tolkien, *The Lord of the Rings*

A twentieth century fantasy trilogy set in Middle-earth in a time before history. It is a story of Good vs. Evil, or Light vs. Darkness, and it involves a Ring that must be destroyed. It has Hobbits, Dwarves, Elves, Wizards, and many other fantastical creatures. Can be read as a Christian allegory.

Leo Tolstoy, *Anna Karenina*

This novel focuses on parallel love stories, one of them adulterous and tragic, the other sanctified by marriage, and thus a blessed, sacramental union. The novel's action moves between two Russian cities: Moscow, a city where good and evil are recognized, and where reconciliation and forgiveness exist; and St. Petersburg, which in contrast, is a city of facades that mask internal complexities, a callous and corrupt city torn away from the divine.

Fyodor Dostoyevsky, *The Brothers Karamazov*

The novel concerns the four sons of Fyodor Karamazov, born of three different mothers. In the course of investigating the father's murder, the reader is led to examine all possible paths for modern Russia, and therefore, humankind. On one level the sons represent different "ways" for humanity: Dmitri, the eldest, depicts the way of the senses; Ivan, the intellect; Alyosha, the soul; and Smerdyakov, the illegitimate son, the debased way of skepticism and secularism. Dostoyevsky sets in motion tenets of the Christian faith as Russian Orthodoxy embodied them, emphasizing the positive effects of suffering, and a belief in the brotherhood of all people. Also embodied in the center of this novel is the message set forth by the character Father Zossima that active love means labor and fortitude.

Aleksandr I. Solzhenitsyn, *A Day in the Life of Ivan Denisovich*

This is a short novel depicting the horrors of the Soviet concentration camps. Its hero, a simple peasant unjustly imprisoned, shows that he will retain his basic humanity no matter what the authorities do to him. Though the reader's attention is focused on one character during one day in one prison camp, it is understood that the story represents all the prisoners in all their days in all the camps. Though the description of the suffering the prisoners endure is mostly in terms of physical deprivation, the moral outrage can be felt as well. Solzhenitsyn is able to articulate his Christian world-view in this novel through a Baptist believer named Alyoshka.

American Classics

James Baldwin, *Go Tell It on the Mountain*

Bringing Harlem and the Black experience to life, this 1953 novel portrays the religious conversion of John Grimes who is frustrated by the fire-and-brimstone theology to which his stepfather subscribes. Focusing on the prayers of the "saints"—John's mother, stepfather, and Aunt Florence—Biblical allusions abound, and set the major conflict, revealing the African-American experience with the Christian religion.

Willa Cather, *Death Comes for the Archbishop*

In 1851 Father Jean Marie Latour comes as the Apostolic Vicar to New Mexico. What he finds are Americans by law, but Mexicans and Indians in custom and belief. In the almost forty years that follow, Latour spreads his faith in an unforgiving landscape, contending with derelict and sometimes rebellious priests, and his own loneliness.

Stephen Crane, *The Red Badge of Courage*

This novella is told through the eyes of Henry Fleming, a young soldier caught up in an unnamed Civil War battle, who is motivated by fear, cowardice, and by egotism. Although nature, in opposition to war, is idealized, the author still infuses his story with religious Christian imagery and metaphors.

Peter De Vries, *The Blood of the Lamb*

Set in the first half of the twentieth century in the Chicago area, this novel is about the search for faith confronted with incurable disease. The first section touches lightly on religion, but is more concerned with the main character, Don Wanderhope's attempts to rise above his middle-class background, which includes his family's Dutch Reform religion. This preoccupation with worldly status is interposed with the concern for religious meaning that forms the focus of the third part of the story. Many of the incidents described in the novel are comic because they illustrate the lack of control people have over their own circumstances. This is the message of the novel, that there is no control, even at the hands of God. There is no deity, Don decides, that can be held responsible for human suffering. God is not responsible for human tragedy, and prayer for the sake of avoiding or alleviating human suffering is pointless. However, DeVries chooses laughter to make most of his points.

Lloyd C. Douglas, *The Robe*

A wealthy Tribune and son of a senator in ancient Rome, Marcellus Gallio, wins Christ's robe as a gambling prize. Knowing that he helped put a man not guilty of any crime to death by crucifixion, he sets forth on a quest to find the truth about the Nazarene's robe, a quest that reaches to the very roots and heart of Christianity, and is set against the vivid background of ancient Rome. Tracing what might have happened to Jesus' robe after the crucifixion, the novel follows characters through the Roman Empire on a journey of adventure, romance, and faith. It is a tale of spiritual longing and ultimate redemption.

Ernest Hemingway, *The Old Man and the Sea*

Deals with an old Cuban fisherman who has eighty-four days without a catch. Far from port on the eighty-fifth day, he hooks a gigantic marlin. Out-matched in the two-day fight, the old man brings the fish alongside and harpoons it. Soon sharks appear, and the old man breaks his knife after he has killed only a few; and during the last night of the voyage home the sharks devour all but the head of the great fish. Can be interpreted as an allegory of man's losing struggle with existence; though the old man fights the great fish with courage and stoicism, he is defeated in the end not by the fish—or by life itself—but by the sharks, or death.

Sinclair Lewis, *Elmer Gantry*

Published in 1927, the novel's title character, who got his first taste of the fame that might have driven the rest of his life while he was attending Terwillinger College in Kansas, starts out as a greedy, shallow, philandering Baptist minister, turns to evangelism, and eventually becomes the leader of a large Methodist congregation. Throughout the novel Gantry encounters fellow religious hypocrites, including Mrs. Evans Riddle, Judson Roberts, and Sharon Falconer, with whom he becomes romantically involved. Although he is often exposed as a fraud, Gantry is never fully discredited. This novel was supposed to be a satiric indictment of the traveling revivals that went from town to town during the early twentieth century.

Herman Melville, *Moby Dick*

Captain Ahab's quest for the white whale becomes a stirring tragedy of vengeance and obsession, a searing parable about humanity lost in a universe of moral ambiguity. A journey in quest of Moby Dick becomes a spiritual quest for truth. It is what his antagonist represents that Ahab fights against. Filled with symbolisms of God and Man.

Herman Melville, *Billy Bud*

Billy Budd and Claggart, the villainous master-at-arms, represent allegorical opposites of good and evil. Captain Vere's decision to hang Billy for slaying the evil Claggart represents the triumph of law. Vere, allegorically the just God of the Old Testament, realizes that his first obligation is to preserve society, not self, so he must condemn Billy to death despite his paternalistic feelings for him. Billy willingly accepts martyrdom, and as the Christ-like Billy mounts the yardarm, the golden sun penetrates the clouds, signifying the hero's resurrection into eternal life.

Tim O'Brien, *The Things They Carried*[1]

Set in Vietnam during the war, this is a profound study of men at war, and the unrelenting images of the things they carried with them and on them—love letters, mine detectors, Bibles, dope, each other—from the actual to the allegoric and metaphoric, a compelling work that finally examines the ethical, moral, and spiritual wars that rage within us all.

---

1. This book contains some offensive language.

Flannery O'Connor, *Wise Blood*

The story of Hazel Motes, a twenty-two-year-old man who is searching for spiritual answers to the questions in his life through an assortment of false prophets, one of which is an itinerant preacher, Asa Hawks, who comes to the Southern town of Taulkinham in order to form "The Church Without Christ," and who ends up dead by the roadside, self-blinded, a human testament to the extremities of insight and zealotry. The irony in the story lies in the fact that every step Hazel thinks will take him farther from Christ, and the religion of his grandfather and mother, simply brings him closer to his Redeemer.

Flannery O'Connor, *The Violent Bear It Away*

Is the tale of Tarwater, a fourteen-year-old prophet who alternately rebels against and succumbs to the religious visions of his uncle.

Harriet Beecher Stowe, *Uncle Tom's Cabin*

More of an abolitionist tract, this lengthy novel argues that slavery as it existed in the United States in the nineteenth century was inhumane and an abomination, and that Christian love and duty demanded an end to it before the injustice and cruelty of slavery brought down on our nation "the wrath of Almighty God!" This "novel," intended to evoke the tears of every American citizen, is filled page after page with both detestable and lovable characters, Christian symbolism, and biblical allusions.

Lew Wallace, *Ben-Hur: A Tale of the Christ*

Set in occupied Jerusalem in the time of Christ, a young Jew feels the crushing weight of the mighty Roman machine, which eventually leads to his being sentenced as a galley slave for life. While his anger fuels his will to survive, a stroke of good fortune changes his status from slave to freeman. From his new position of wealth and prestige, Ben-Hur plots his vengeance on those who have wronged him and his beloved mother and sister. However, an unusual man named Jesus, who perhaps is the promised Messiah, begins to trouble Ben-Hur's mind, and his strange teachings of humility, forgiveness, and love for one's enemies upset the vengeful plans Ben-Hur has so carefully devised.

Great Poets and Poetry

Matthew Arnold, (1822–1888); "Dover Beach"

Written after the publication of Darwin's *Origin of the Species;* the speaker in this poem laments the loss of religious faith, and seeing the world now as dark and filled with violence, turns to his love as the only possible avenue of finding hope, meaning, and happiness.

William Blake (1757–1827)

British poet, artist, and mystic who created his own beliefs from Christianity and various philosophies.

Anne Bradstreet *(*1612–1672*)*

An American Puritan poet who immigrated to New England with her husband who became governor of Massachusetts. She brought up 8 children in conditions of hardship.

Thomas Carlisle (Twentieth Century)

American Presbyterian pastor and poet.

Emily Dickinson (1830–1886)

Was born in Amhurst, Massachusetts, received her education at Mount Holyoke Seminary, though she lived out her life unmarried in her parents' home, mostly as a recluse; she wrote more than 1,000 lyrics, all but only 7 of which were published after her death.

John Donne (1572–1631)

Was born in England; became an Anglican Priest, and quickly earned a reputation as one of the greatest preachers of his time.

T. S. Eliot, *Four Quartets*

Published in 1943, the Quartets are four related poems said to have been modeled on the late quartets of Beethoven. They are both a record of the journey from skepticism to faith and an attempt to communicate a religious experience in an age lacking traditional religious belief.

George Herbert, (1593-1633); "Virtue"

Explores the differences between the transient worldly things and the immortal soul.) and "Easter Wings" (A shaped verse in the form of a petitional prayer, in which the speaker asks the Lord to permit him to sing praises and to feel the joy of the Easter victory over sin.

Gerard Manley Hopkins (1844–1889)

Was ordained a Jesuit priest and served in missions in London, Liverpool, Oxford, and Glasgow from 1877–1882. He was also a Professor of Greek at University College in Dublin. His early poems celebrate the beauty of God's world.

John Milton, (1608-1674)
"When I Consider How My Light Is Spent"

The speaker complains about his failures and frustrations, only one of which is blindness. More significant is the crisis of faith in which the speaker expresses uncertainty about God's expectations, and assumes that he will be rejected.

Francis Thompson,, (1859–1907)
"The Hound of Heaven" and other poems

Was born in England to devout Catholic parents. He was addicted to opium, which induced in him the creative visions for which he longed. Leaving behind his studies in medicine due to his more literary disposition, he lived a life of poverty and desperation. He wrote many poems about faith, but this one is his most famous, concerning the hunt by the Dogs of God for men's souls.

Poetry Anthology

Mary Batchelor, *Poetry for the Soul:*
700 Best Loved Christian Poems

A collection of 250 poets from a variety of ages and cultures, presenting both classic and contemporary verse that will nourish the soul.

Short Stories

Nathaniel Hawthorne, "Young Goodman Brown"

Filled with Christian symbolism, this is an allegorical story about a young Puritan who journeys into the forest one night in a dream, only to come out realizing that he can no longer accept faith in other's righteousness, and thus in God, because he has learned through an encounter with Satan that man is fallen and is inherently evil, and the Puritan doctrine of election, along with everything else, has been a lie.

James Joyce, "Araby"

The theme is the shattering of an ideal, youthful and childish love, but the imagery is heavily religious and angelic against a setting which seems to lack any life in it at all.

Ursula K. Le Guin, "The Ones Who Walk Away from Amelas"

The narrator depicts a pastoral, utopian society where everyone is happy, where there exist few laws, no military, no clergy, no machines, and no guilt. Then she asks the reader, "Do you believe?" Before she describes the unjust wretchedness of one innocent child condemned to physical and emotional torture, who represents a scapegoat, carrying all the dark, emotional debris of the society, thus purifying it.

Flannery O'Connor, "A Good Man is Hard to Find"

This story is grounded in situational irony, involving conflict between ordinary folks who are on a family trip to Florida, chance in the form of an accident, and evil in the form of the Misfit, a psychopathic killer with whom the grandmother tries to talk about the need for Jesus and redemption, primarily as a means of saving herself from certain death.

Katherine Anne Porter, "The Jilting of Granny Weatherall"

Granny is on her deathbed, and significant events of her life are flashing through her mind. The plot is concerned with the conflict between Granny and death, and the lifelong conflict between her and adversity which began when she was jilted on her wedding day, and continued with the deaths of her young daughter and then later her husband, all of which she has come through with dignity, and thus she is portrayed throughout the story as a giver of light. However, the jilting, and the parallels between the earthly and heavenly bridegroom, are linked in Granny's mind. That the bridegroom appears neither on her wedding day or her death day, is an extreme disappointment—both an earthly and spiritual jilting, all the more so because a priest was present on both occasions.

Frank O'Connor, "First Confession"

This story takes a comic and good-natured, though satiric look at the sternness and rigidity of religion. The story presents a series of mounting crises, namely, a family squabble, the fear of hell as described by Mrs. Ryan, the narrator's hesitancy to go to confession, and the farcical actions in the church. The climax is the confession itself, which sets the narrator's apprehensions aside, due to an amused but sympathetic priest. The conflict of the plot can be described as punishment vs. forgiveness, anger vs. toleration, rigidity vs. understanding, or the letter of the law vs. the spirit of the law.

O. Henry, "The Gift of the Magi"

The title refers to the three wise men in the Bible who were led by a star to the baby Jesus, bringing valuable gifts, though not to a baby. This story is about a young couple who at Christmastime find themselves without money to buy the other a gift, and thus they each sell their most valuable possessions in order to buy what they think the other would most like to have.

Ernest Hemingway, "A Clean, Well-Lighted Place"

The cafe becomes a symbol for created meaning in an otherwise dark universe devoid of God. A negation of the Lord's Prayer is cited by one of the waiters: "Our nothing who art in nothing, nothing be thy name . . ." Even in a universe stripped of meaning, man needs to find order.

Jorge Luis Borges, "The Gospel According to Mark"

A young man from Buenos Aires is trapped by a flood on an isolated ranch. To pass the time he reads the Gospel to a family with unforeseen results.

Gabriel Garcia Marquez, "A Very Old Man With Enormous Wings"

A worn-out old angel crashes in Pelayo's seaside yard. His dilemma is whether to sell tickets or call a priest.

Bernard Malamud, "Angel Levine"

Broke, ill, and desperate, the tailor Manischevitz begs God for help. But when he discovers a black man in his living room that claims to be a Jewish angel, the tailor refuses to believe.

Leo Tolstoy, "The Death of Ivan Llych"

In order to establish the nature of the antihuman society in which Ivan has lived, Tolstoy begins the story immediately after Ivan's death. For his friends, his death means the possibility of promotion; for his wife, it means a grant of money from the government. It is not until he faces death that Ivan realizes his life has been actuated by the same superficial, calculating concerns, and that he has been unable to establish a vital or meaningful relationship with others. The one person who becomes the antithesis of everything Ivan's life represents is a young peasant lad named Gerasim, who helps him to bring into question the very meaning of life. Finally, after much physical suffering and mental anguish, Ivan is brought through the "black hole" of utter despair and into the "light." This symbolic rebirth is mystical, and Christian, and releases Ivan from terror and doubt. He is flooded with feelings of pity and forgiveness for those around him, but more significantly, he accepts total responsibility for his own life, thus recognizing that it is he who must ask forgiveness of others.

Drama

Sophocles, *Oedipus Rex*

A Greek play which raises the question of whether the downfall of Oedipus, King of Thebes, was a result of fate, that is, forces beyond his control, or due to aspects of his character which led to errors in judgment and action. The city of Thebes is under a curse because of a sin committed long ago by one of its citizens. King Oedipus, who once saved the city from the Sphinx, has vowed to get to the bottom of it and to make everything right, but in so doing he uncovers a revelation that points the finger at him. It is pride, haughtiness, sacrilege, unholiness, and injustice, which implicate him in the horror that is finally revealed. The central conflict is either Oedipus against the gods, or against himself.

Everyman

An anonymous morality play written about 1485; the central character Everyman, who stands for every Christian person, is confronted with Death, who comes to Everyman in the midst of his idleness and ignorance. Pleading for time to prepare for death, Everyman asks for support from Fellowship, Kindred and Cousin, and Goods (wealth), but they all refuse. After self-searching he then turns to Knowledge and Good Deeds.

Robert Bolt, *A Man For All Seasons*

The story of Sir Thomas More, a strong Catholic, who was a long-time friend and Lord Chancellor to Henry VIII. When Henry broke with the Church in 1531 after the Pope refused to grant him a divorce, More, refusing to take an oath acknowledging the supremacy of England's king over all foreign sovereigns—including the Pope, was imprisoned, and finally executed in 1535.

T. S. Eliot, *Murder in the Cathedral*

This 1935 play deals with the assassination of Thomas Becket. It reveals the politics, both temporal and churchly that lay behind the murder. He presents the archbishop as a man torn between acting and suffering. Most of the play is in poetic form.

Johann Wolfgang von Goethe, *Faust*

Written in the 1700s, this is the story of a disillusioned scholar, who turns to search the world of experience when his intellectual pursuits become dry and lifeless. Nearing despair, he makes a pact with the devil, Mephisto, so that he will be given infinite knowledge with godlike power to last until he reaches a stage of satisfaction. If he ever declares, "Oh stay; you are so fair!" to any given moment, he will immediately be required to surrender his soul to the devil. The play continues as Faust, who doesn't believe in God, falls in love with a deeply religious girl named Gretchen, whom he seduces. Unable to live with her sins she kills her and Faust's child and is sentenced to death. However, recognizing her guilt, she is in the end saved by God, whereas Faust escapes and continues on with a series of temptations throughout the world of time that take him to the brink of moral degradation.

Christopher Marlowe, *Dr. Faustus*

Written in the 1500s, it tells the story of a medieval scientist who allies himself with the devil, who promises to serve Faust in this world, until Faust can serve him in hell. The doctor doubts his choices many times during his twenty-four year bargain, but remains firm in the belief that God has already condemned him, so he continues to follow the devil and has the time of his life when he is provided with fun and all the riches of the world. However, at the end, Faust realizes that all his experiences were not worth his soul, and begs God to save him, but then it is no longer possible. The devil tears his body apart and takes his soul with him to infinite sufferings.

Arthur Miller, *The Crucible*

This is about the witch-hunts and trials of the seventeenth century in Salem, Massachusetts. Based on historical people and real events, it portrays a community engulfed by hysteria, fears and suspicions, and self-righteousness.

John Pielmeier, *Agnes of God*

This play has only three characters: a nun, a psychiatrist, and a novice, but it deals with the very risqué subject matter of abortion when a dead baby is found in a trash can.

Thornton Wilder, *Our Town*

Covering three periods in the history of the small village of Grover's Corners, New Hampshire, this drama is about finding out after it is too late that those of us living never realize life as we live it, that most of us spend our time on this earth in ignorance and blindness.

Contemporary Fiction (by Secular Publishers)

Mitch Albom, *The Five People You Meet in Heaven*

An 83-year-old craggy war veteran has felt that he has spent most of his life trapped in a meaningless and lonely existence working at maintaining the rides at an amusement park. However, on this particular day, Eddie will be killed when the cable snaps on one of the new rides. The last person he will see will be a little girl whose life he was trying to save. Their hands touch, and then nothing. He awakes in the afterlife to find that five people, loved ones and strangers alike, will show up to explain to him the meaning of his existence, and how each one of them had changed the course of his life.

Harriette Arnow, *The Dollmaker*

Gertie Nevels' peaceful life in the Kentucky hills is uprooted when she and her family are thrust into the confusion and violent assimilation of World War II Detroit, where her husband has found work in a factory. Gertie has to battle fiercely and relentlessly to protect those things she holds most precious—her children, her heritage, and her ability to create beauty in the suffocating shadow of ugliness and despair. Intertwined in this is the conflict between the competitive visions of God, God as love and God as vengeance. In a bitter irony, Gertie becomes a Judas, betraying the Christly figure in the piece of wood she never has enough time to carve out. There are means of salvation— love, especially of her children, and art, but neither one have a place in a world of daily, bitter struggle.

Olive Anne Burns, *Cold Sassy Tree*

Cold Sassy, Georgia in 1906, had never been a whirlpool of excitement. If the preacher's wife's petticoat showed, the ladies would make the talk last a week, until one day E. Rucker Blakeslee, proprietor of the general store and barely three weeks a widower, eloped with Miss Love Simpson, a woman half his age, and a Yankee! That's when fourteen-year-old Will Tweedy's adventures begin, and a pious town came to life.

Douglas Coupland, *Life After God*[2]

This author, who in his first novel coined the term *Generation X*, has written this shorter collection of stories that take a look at the first genera-

---

2. This book contains some offensive language.

tion raised without religion, who as they grow older become disenchanted with the world of TV, malls, fast food, and all the hype of modern living. Where do a person's "religious impulses" flow when they have no belief system to sustain them? How does one cope with loneliness, anxiety, and broken relationships? These stories offer a bleak glimpse into a world they may or may not recognize.

E. L. Doctorow, *City of God*[3]

This is a novel about faith and doubt, science and religion, and the quest for a believable God at the end of the twentieth century. It's about the Holocaust and the possibilities for holiness in a secular world. It's about popular music and the making of movies. It's about spiritual emptiness, the rational mind, and messianic longing.

Garrison Keillor, *Lake Wobegon Days*

Starting with the town's early history from the Unitarian missionaries, to its crazed founder, to the Norwegian Lutherans and German Catholics, it moves on to the narrator's own memories growing up as a Sanctified Brethren in the 1940s and 50s. The story is filled with memorable characters and places that become a portrait of small town life in America.

Norman Maclean, *A River Runs Through It*[4]

This novella recalls the experiences of a young man in frontier Montana, of his minister father who taught his sons religion and fly fishing, and of his brother, an artist at trout fishing but less than successful at life.

Norman Mailer, *The Gospel According to the Son*

A daring attempt to retell the story of Jesus in Jesus' own words, though in a relaxed style, plus a re-creation of the world through which Jesus walked.

Catherine Marshall, *Christy*

Set in Cutter Gap, Tennessee beginning in 1912, this is a moving story of a nineteen year old girl who goes to the Cove to be a teacher, but learns

3. This work models the postmodern novel, experimenting with both narrative and structure, as well as demonstrating man's struggle to understand and accept the traditional view of God. It contains some offensive language and an offensive scene.
4. This book contains some offensive language.

more herself from the people she meets there. Other characters include Alice Henderson, a Quaker mission worker, David Grantland, a young minister, and Neil MacNeill, a physician of the Cove.

Jodi Picoult, *Keeping Faith*[5]

Mariah White catches her husband with another woman, and Faith, their seven-year-old daughter, witnesses every painful minute. In the aftermath of a sudden divorce, Mariah struggles with depression, and Faith begins to confide in an imaginary friend. But when Faith, a girl with no religious background, starts reciting passages from the Bible, develops stigmata, and begins to perform miraculous healings, Mariah wonders if her daughter might actually be seeing God. Before it's over, they become plagued by a media circus, organized religion, and a battle for custody.

Chaim Potok, *My Name is Asher Lev*

A story about a religious boy with an overwhelming need to draw, to paint, to render the world he knows and the pain he feels for everyone to see. A loner, Asher has an extraordinary God-given gift that cannot be controlled, but that possesses a spirit all its own, yet it is a gift he must learn to master without shaming his people or relinquishing any part of his deeply felt Judaism.

Anne Rice, *Christ the Lord Out of Egypt: A Novel*

This is a fictionalized account told in the first person narrative voice of Jesus when he was seven years old. It chronicles his family's journey from Egypt to Judea as they get caught up in the revolution that follows the death of King Herod. During this time he learns about his divine heritage, and experiments with his mysterious healing powers. The novel contains authentic historical and cultural details, as Rice stays as true to the biblical account as possible. She also uses several extra-biblical sources, including The Infant Gospel of Thomas for the details of the legendary events described in her story concerning his turning a clay dove into a real one, and his bringing back to life a school friend. While this book may upset some readers, because of the liberties that Rice takes, it is worthwhile noting that this once atheist author of the Vampire Chronicles converted to Christianity while she conducted research for this book, which she discusses in great detail at the end of the novel. She says that she hopes that

5. This book contains some offensive language.

people who never knew Christ will want to find out more about him after reading her book, and that she has committed the remainder of her life to only writing books that honor God!

Lee Smith, *Saving Grace*[6]

Set in the North Carolina and Tennessee mountains, this novel examines religious faith, sin and salvation, and signs and wonders among snake-handling, tongues-talking, scripture-quoting ecstatics of Appalachia.

Nicholas Sparks, *A Walk to Remember*[7]

It was 1958, and Landon Carter, a senior at Beaufort High, thought the last person in town he'd ever fall for would be Jamie Sullivan, the daughter of the town's Baptist minister. She was a quiet girl who always carried a Bible with her schoolbooks, content to live apart from the other teens. It was a twist of fate that made Jamie his partner for the homecoming dance, and Landon's life would never be the same.

Nancy E. Turner, *These is My Words: The Diary of Agnes Prine, 1881–1901*

This is a story about one woman's struggle to endure the hardships in the Arizona Territory. Filled with references to religion, there is evidence that religious teaching influenced each character in the novel, both practically and spiritually.

Young Adult Fiction
(Also recommended for adult readers!)

Peter S. Beagle, *The Last Unicorn*

The unicorn discovers that she may be the last unicorn in the world, and sets off on a journey that will forever change her life. Along the way she meets Schmendrick, an inept magician—when he rescues her from Mommy Fortuna's Midnight Carnival, where only some of the mythical beasts displayed are illusions. An old but kindly spinster, and even a heroic prince join them. Ahead wait the evil King Haggard and his Red Bull, who has imprisoned all the other unicorns by driving them into the sea. The

6. This book contains some offensive language.
7. This book contains some offensive language.

only way the unicorn can save the others is by turning into something else, so the magician turns her into a human. However, as the unicorn becomes more human, she forgets her mission, yet through everything she learns to love, cry, and even regret. Beagle argues brilliantly for the need for magic in our lives and the folly of forgetting to dream.

Frances Hodgson Burnett, *The Secret Garden*

At home in England, a troubled orphan named Mary, her spoiled bedridden cousin Colin, and a kind country boy called Dikon discover a splendid garden hidden behind a locked door. Rich in symbolic imagery, this secret garden shows the children beauty, friendship, and a new reality that contrasts sharply with their bleak past.

Michael Ende, *The Neverending Story*

This is a magical tale of a lonely, solitary boy who steps through the pages of a book into a special kingdom. There, in an imaginary land, on a dangerous quest to save the life of the Childlike Empress and the entire world of Fantastica, Bastian learns the true measure of his own courage, and that even he has the capacity to love. This story teaches all of us to never stop using our imaginations.

Anne Frank, *The Diary of a Young Girl*

She died in the concentration camp of Bergen-Belsen in 1945, but her diary, found on the floor of her family's hiding place in Amsterdam, is an intimate and revealing commentary of a girl who from age thirteen to age fifteen wrote about both her family and her inner life, while living in isolation and in fear of the Nazis.

Dorothy Gilman, *The Maze in the Heart of the Castle*

Colin's parents both died in the plague, so scared, confused, and angry, he seeks out a monk who tells him about a haunted castle on Rheembeck Mountain, and the old wizard who lives there. Perhaps Colin could find a way to stop his pain. But once inside the ancient stone maze that leads to a mystical land, there can be no going back. It will be a journey that will change him forever.

Brian Jacques, *Redwall*

Book 1 in the *Redwall* series, begins in the Summer of the Late Rose, when to the inhabitants of Redwall Abbey, especially to Matthias, a clumsy, orphaned mouse, things seem quiet and peaceful. However, Cluny the Scourge, the evil one-eyed rat warlord, is determined to destroy the tranquility as he prepares to fight a bloody battle for ownership of Redwall. Meanwhile, Matthias is trying to prove his worth, and gets a little bit of help from the spirit of Martin the Warrior, founder of Redwall. This series, which is magical and mystical, contains the stuff of legends—of good battling with, and ultimately triumphing over evil.

Madeleine L'Engle, *A Wrinkle in Time*

Meg Murray's father had been experimenting with the fifth dimension of time travel when he mysteriously disappeared. Now Meg, her brother Charles Wallace, and her friend Calvin have to go rescue him, but they must outwit the forces of evil they will encounter on their journey.

Madeleine L'Engle, *A Swiftly Tilting Planet* and *A Wind in the Door.*

Madeleine L'Engle is also known as a twentieth century American poet as well as an award-winning writer of children's books, converted from atheism, and was writer-in-residence at the Cathedral of St. John the Divine in New York.

C. S. Lewis, *The Chronicles of Narnia*

Seven books written in a fairy-tale mode, containing such overtly Christian themes as sacrifice, death and resurrection, the nature of evil, the measure of faith, the divine creation and ending of a world, and the quest for the divine. They contain contemporary children, a wardrobe, talking beasts, a lamppost, a lion, and many other diverse and extraordinary phenomena.

Naomi Shihab Nye, *Habibi*

This is a story about a young girl named Liyana, whose father decides to move their family from St. Louis to Palestine, where he grew up. Though her grandmother, Sitti, and the rest of her relatives live in the West Bank, she knows very little about her family's Arab heritage. They are strangers, and speak a language she doesn't understand. It isn't until she meets Omer, a Jewish boy her age, that her homesickness fades. However, everything discourages the friendship between the two. Ultimately this becomes a story of hope, that peace could come in the hearts of the young, if it were nourished. The book is also rich with Mediterranean Arab/Jewish culture.

The author and Shihab Nye in Charleston, WV, 2004.

Rainer Maria Rilke, *Letters To a Young Poet*

Possibly the most famous and beloved letters of the twentieth century, they were written when Rilke was himself still a young man with most of his greatest works still before him. They are addressed to a nineteen-year-old military student who has sent Rilke some of his poetry after discovering that Rilke had attended this same military school, a period in Rilke's life to which he referred as "one long terrifying damnation." The young man asks for advice about becoming a writer. While the two never met, over a period of several years Rilke responded with these letters, almost as if he were reaching back to his own younger self, offering advice and deep spiritual insight on art, love, personal fulfillment, solitude, and creativity.

Antoine de Saint-Exupery, *The Little Prince*

This is a fable about a prince whose plane is forced down in the Sahara, a thousand miles from help. He encounters a stranger who says, "If you please, draw me a sheep," and thus begins the remarkable history of the little prince who lived alone on a tiny planet no larger than a house. But while on Earth he learns from a fox the secret of what is really important in life.

Ian Serraillier, *Escape From Warsaw*

Based on a true story of real events and real families, this story centers around three children, who in 1942, watch as their mother is arrested by Nazi Storm Troopers, leaving them completely alone and having to fend for themselves. Learning that their father, who had previously been taken away to a concentration camp, has escaped and made it to Switzerland, they begin their own long and dangerous trip out of Warsaw, fearing that they may never see their parents again. I read this book thirty years ago, and never forgot the impression it made on me!

J. R. R. Tolkien, *The Hobbit*

Bilbo Baggins was a Hobbit who wanted to be left alone until Gandalf, a wizard, came along with a band of dwarves, drawing Bilbo into their quest to confront the great dragon, Smaug, and recapture their stolen treasure. This adventurous fantasy sees Bilbo go through many changes before he is able to return to his home in the peaceful Shire.

Some Great Contemporary Mythic Fiction
(by Christian Publishers)

Donna Fletcher Crow, *Glastonbury*

This saga of faith and history follows the birth of Christianity to its arrival in Britain, and its development, beginning with Celtic Britain, Roman Britain, Arthurian Britain, and then as it later became known as Anglo-Saxon England, Norman England, and then Tudor England. Glastonbury becomes "the symbol of faith so ancient that only legend can describe its origin." As the legacy of faith is passed from generation to generation, each era of believers found refuge in Glastonbury, including St. George and St. Patrick during their captivity under the Roman Empire, King Arthur, St. Augustine of Canterbury in the midst of the Dark Ages, as well as during the upheaval under the rule of Henry VIII that led to the Reformation. Though there were dark times during each period, faith, trust, and risk rekindled the light.

Stephen Lawhead, *Taliesin*

As Germanic tribes free the Isle of Britain from its Roman conquerors, the legend of Taliesin is born. Taliesin falls in love with Princess Charis, and together they have a son, Merlin, who grows up to become the fabled magician at the court of King Arthur. *Taliesin* sets the stage for an original Arthurian rendition. The legends of King Arthur come alive with a Christian world-view in this masterfully told series, The Pendragon Cycle, of which *Taliesin* is the first book. Also read *Byzantium*.

Young Aidan is one of a small band of Irish monks chosen to accompany a magnificent illuminated manuscript, splendidly covered with silver and jewels, across the sea to Byzantium. There, the gift will be presented to the emperor, who will then be predisposed to hear of the difficulties facing the Irish church. But before reaching landfall in Brittany, the monks' coracle is set upon by Viking raiders who capture Aidan and take him into slavery in their northern homeland. The Book of Kells does survive, and Aidan is able to fulfill his quest. However, before it's over not only is there a Viking raid on Byzantium, but there is an expedition to the Holy Land, imprisonment in a desert prison-mine, wars at sea, and even more adventures before the monks' commission is discharged.

Also read *The Paradise War* (the first of a series involving Celtic fantasy).

George MacDonald, *Phantastes*

A thrilling story of the narrator's adventures in fairyland, where he confronts tree spirits, sojourns to the palace of the fairy queen, and searches for the spirit of the earth.

Also read *Lilith:* A story of Mr. Vane, an orphan and heir to a large house in which he has a vision that leads him through an old mirror into another world, where he hauntingly explores the ultimate mystery of evil.

Walter Wangerin, Jr., *The Book of the Dun Cow*

An allegorical fantasy, or animal fable, that ferociously pits good against evil in a time when animals could speak, and when Chauntecleer the Rooster ruled over a peaceful kingdom, until the evil monster Wyrm began to break free from beneath the earth. Continued in *The Book of Sorrows.*

Walter Wangerin, Jr., *The Orphean Passages*

The story of a Christian pastor's career and the drama of his faith, interlaced with the classical myth of Orpheus and Eurydice, paralleling the twists and turns all must follow in their journeys of faith.

Memoirs/Autobiographies

Maya Angelou, *I Know Why the Caged Bird Sings*

The first in a series of five autobiographical works, this book chronicles Marguerite Johnson's, and her brother Bailey's journey at ages four and five to Stamps, Arkansas, where they are sent to live with their strong and loving grandmother, and handicapped uncle. While living in the segregated deep south, she learns a lot from this exceptional woman and from the tightly knit black community. The lessons she learns, and her strong faith carry her through the hardships she endures later on in her life, including a sexual assault when she was eight, and an unwanted pregnancy at age sixteen. Both she and her brother are transported back and forth from Arkansas to St. Louis to live with their mother, to California. As she comes of age she must battle feelings of insecurity, inferiority, and ugliness. Written by one of the most beloved black women and poets of our time, this book should touch everyone's heart! It does contain some graphic details, written in order to portray the pain and suffering the author underwent.

Frederick Buechner, *The Sacred Journey*

Believing that God speaks into our personal lives, Buechner has observed, "all theology, like all fiction, is at its heart autobiography." He says that we are all part of a divine comedy, and that we should never question the truth of what we fail to understand, for the world is filled with wonders. This is the story of his own journey into faith as a child, looking back on it as a man who had passed the age of fifty. Buechner is an ordained Presbyterian minister and the author of thirty works of fiction and nonfiction. His work has been nominated for the Pulitzer Prize and the National Book Award, and the American Academy and Institute of Arts and Letters have honored him.

Annie Dillard, *An American Childhood*

Takes a loving and nostalgic look back at her childhood, growing up in Pittsburgh during the 1950s. She recalls her interest in nature and the visible world "turning [her] curious to books." She also captures the pain of being raised by two slightly odd parents who did not want her growing up narrow-minded because of too much money and pampering.

Natalie Goldberg, *The Great Failure:*
A Bartender, a Monk, and My Unlikely Path to Truth

One of America's favorite authors on writing, inspiring millions to approach it in a Zen-like way, writes about her own life's journey, which had been predominately influenced by her father and her Zen teacher. It explores the love and betrayal she experienced by each, and how she transformed her feelings into courage, compassion, and forgiveness. I also highly recommend her books on writing and the writing life: *Writing Down the Bones, Wild Mind: Living the Writer's Life,* and *Thunder and Lightening: Cracking Open the Writer's Craft.*

bell hooks, *Bone Black: Memories of a Girlhood*

[H]ooks, born Gloria Watkins (she took her great-grandmother's name, but writes it in lower case), chronicles her life growing up in rural Kentucky, as an heir to poverty and racism, surrounded by people too wrapped up in their own struggles to offer her much help. She writes of her mother suffering an abusive marriage, of her siblings' rejection of her for being "different," of her own painful discovery of sexuality, and how she turned to religion and books for escape. It is a very moving coming of age story written by a woman who believes there are not enough autobiographies written by black women authenticating the black experience.

Sue Monk Kidd, *The Dance of the Dissident Daughter*

Is the author of *The Secret Life of Bees* and *firstlight,* a collection of her early inspirational writings. Once a thriving Christian author, Kidd began to question conventional religion and her role as a woman within its confines. She explains the emptiness she felt, and takes a journey away from Christianity into a spirituality that speaks more directly to women. Hers is a journey backwards into myth and the goddess. It's worthwhile reading for any woman who wants to understand the feminine side of the soul, and what one step-by-step spiritual search looks like.

Anne Lamott, *Traveling Mercies: Some Thoughts on Faith*

Having entered into Christian faith through the back door of depression and alcoholism, Anne explores with a lot of wit her quirky walk with faith and how, against all odds, she came to believe in God. If you're looking for squeaky-clean Christianity and a conservative theology, this book is not for you. However, what I believe it does is shed light on how wonderful it is when anyone comes to Christ, and how instrumental an accepting church family can be in helping a broken person heal. In her sequel, *Plan B: Further Thoughts on Faith* Lamott takes the reader on her day-to-day struggle with living out her faith in a world filled with terrorism, war, Alzheimer's, and the passing of friends.

Madeleine L'Engle, *The Circle of Quiet*

A prolific author of books for children and adults, she has written three books that make up the Crosswicks Journal, of which this is the first. Reading this book is like having a conversation with a wise friend. She traverses a vast territory of topics, including creativity, inspiration, and the necessity of writing, to questions that have plagued her about faith and God. She discusses her own personal failures, domestic life, food, sex, the counter-culture, the effect of the changing nature of education and language on America's youth, the community, solitude, listening, talking, and reading.

Catherine Marshall, *Meeting God at Every Turn*

As the author of the best-selling novel *Christy*, Marshall tells stories that let us glimpse not only into her life, but also into the character of God. From recollections of childhood memories to the death of her first husband, and from raising children to becoming a grandmother, she recounts how God provided unfailing love and sufficient grace at every step.

Kathleen Norris, *Dakota: A Spiritual Geography*

Norris writes about a place in the Plains of Middle America as though living there were equal to living a monastic life. Since 1980 the economy and the population of the Dakotas have fallen, and the people have gotten stuck in the tension between myth and truth. But as St. Hilary, a fourth century bishop once wrote, "Everything that seems empty is full of the angels of God." And so if you find city life and industrialization hard to stomach, this deeply spiritual book about what there is to see and touch in a land so vast it seems more like an ocean than earth will touch your heart.

Kathleen Norris, *The Cloister Walk*

In this book, which is part memoir and part meditation, Norris explains how a woman from a Protestant background, who often has more doubt than faith, can be drawn to the ancient practice of monasticism. This is part record of her time spent with the Benedictines, and part meditation on various aspects of monastic life and how its liturgy, its ritual, and its sense of community can impart meaning and deepen our secular lives.

Mary Swander, *The Desert Pilgrim:*
En Rout to Mysticism and Miracles

In this inspiring memoir, Swander recalls driving home one cold winter night, and being struck by a car, an accident that left her almost complete-ly paralyzed and in chronic pain. A lapsed Catholic, without any family to speak of, and now severely disabled, she was suddenly faced with how very alone she was in the world. She recounts her journey as she travels to New Mexico in search of an alternative medicine, and emotional, physical, and spiritual recovery amid the stark desert of the American southwest. She meets a Russian Orthodox monk who helps restore her faith, and a *curandera*, whose herbal remedies help restore her body. As she chronicles her own transcendent experiences, Swander investigates the history of healing as well as mystics such as Teresa of Avila, St. Francis of Assisi, and Hildegard of Bingen.

Luci Swindoll, *I Married Adventure:*
Looking at Life Through the Lens of Possibility

This is a book that makes me *not* feel like I have to apologize for loving travel and adventure! To her adventure is "an attitude, not a behavior." She reveals how she learned to capture each moment, as well as how she learned to celebrate and live life to the fullest, and with God's blessing! She explains how God has given us a spirit of curiosity, and an ability to dream that can lift us right out of mediocrity and boredom. She insists that if we listen to our hearts God will send us on an adventure that will fill our lives with wonder and delight better than anything we could have imagined. She weaves throughout the tale of her own life growing up, attending col-lege, and working thirty years at Mobil Corporation her adventure stories of travels around the world, spiced up with some amazing tidbits of insight into living a spiritual life that combines heart and mind.

Spiritual Journeys and Travel Writing

A Woman's Path: Women's Best Spiritual Travel Writing

A collection of stories from Travelers' Tales that narrates the passion of women's pilgrimage and journey. Written by Anne Lamott, Linda Ellerbee, Natalie Goldberg, Diane Ackerman, Maya Angelou, and many others, they are stories of discovery, awakening, and personal transformation all woven into tales of travel.

Anthony DeStefano, *A Travel Guide to Heaven*

Not since C. S. Lewis wrote *The Great Divorce* has an author so enthusiastically invited readers to imagine what heaven might be like. And like Lewis' idea of heaven as a place of joy, DeStafano's look at heaven involves fun too. Wanting to divorce the image of heaven from the dreamlike, ethereal image it has been given by many poets and theologians down through the centuries, he portrays it as a place that will be dynamic and physical, exciting, interesting, and uplifting. Using the Bible as his guide, DeStafano sets out to look for clues, and invites us all to get our travel bags ready.

Bruce Feiler, *Walking the Bible:* *A Journey By Land Through the Five Books of Moses*

This has been described as one man's epic odyssey through the greatest stories ever told, one that grounds the Bible in both soil and history. A must read for anyone who has ever wondered about the region of the land of the Old Testament. Visiting in Mesopotamia, or modern Iraq, traveling to Turkey and then to Egypt, onto Jordan, and into Israel, Feiler is driven by his own curiosity and questions as he follows the trail of the Jewish fathers.

Katherine Kurs, editor, *Searching for Your Soul:* *Writers of Many Faiths Share Their Personal Stories* *of Spiritual Discovery*

This is a collection of stories and essays by more than 50 writers who undertake to explore the "rough terrain" that is their own spiritual journey. The writers are Jewish, Hindu, Muslim, Protestant, Roman Catholic, Mormon, Buddhist, Pagan, and Jehovah Witness. Topics include ancestors and traditions, secrets and revelations, flesh and spirit, suffering and mortality, and exploration and encounter. The message is that to undertake spiritual living is not to invite smooth sailing! Almost any reader will find stories with which they may relate, while others will simply enlarge or challenge your thinking.

Modern Christian Mystics

Thomas Merton, *New Seeds of Contemplation* and *No Man Is An Island*

"Without a life of the spirit," Merton maintains, "our whole existence becomes unsubstantial and illusory. The life of the spirit, by integrating us in the real order established by God, puts us in the fullest possible contact with reality – not as we imagine it, but as it really is." Both works are a series of stimulating spiritual reflections on contemplation, holiness, union, solitude, pureness of heart, hatred, faith, wisdom, obedience, liberty, detachment, prayer, love, and a host of other topics beneficial to anyone who is struggling to find the meaning of human existence and to live a rich, full, and noble life.

Thomas Moore, *Care of the Soul: A Guide for Cultivating Depth and Sacredness in Everyday Life*

While Moore is not technically a mystic, his first book is basically a spiritual primer, which explains to many of us what we already know. However, for many involved in traditional religion, it must be read with a contemplative heart, rather than dissected intellectually. Moore says that true spirituality involves trying to accept our humanity rather than trying to transcend it. He explains that feeding our souls, at least as much as we feed our minds and our bodies, will help to cultivate dignity, peace, and depth of character. In his companion volume, *The Soul's Religion: Cultivating a Profoundly Spiritual Way of Life*, Moore takes spiritual teachings out of different texts, temples, and churches, and applies them to everyday life. He draws not only from Christianity, Zen, and Taoism, but from many literary authors and poets as well. Again, even if a reader cannot agree with everything Moore says, it's difficult not to be challenged by him.

Simone Weil, *Waiting for God*

Born in Paris in 1909, she earned a *baccalaureat es letters* with distinction at the age of fifteen. She then went on to study philosophy, which she qualified to teach in 1931. In 1941 a friend introduced her to the Reverend Father Perrin, at the same time her mystical tendencies and her preoccupation with the notion of God became more pronounced, leading her to write pages on the "Our Father" and on the Love of God. This collection of letters and essays emerge from thought-provoking discussions and correspondence she had with Reverend Father Perrin, and contains meditations on the relationship of human life to the realm of the transcendent. She speaks of the problem of belief, and on the doctrines of the Church. She remained, however, an outsider to organized religion. Thus she speaks as an outsider to outsiders, a special kind of saint.

Contemporary Literature from Around the World (all genres)

Etel Adnan, *Sitt Marie Rose*

This very short novel is the story of a woman abducted by militiamen during the Civil War in Lebanon and executed. Told through a variety of narrative voices, it reveals the tribal mentality to which Arabs identify so strongly, and which makes the Middle East a dangerous powerhouse. It explores the Lebanese Christian right who is at war with Islam, the Palestinian refugee militants, and other groups who all live in fear of the daily kidnappings and tortures of passers-by. It is also about the rape and destruction of Beirut.

Mariama Ba, *So Long a Letter*

Her first novel is a sequence of reminiscences, some happy, some bitter, recounted by a Senegalese schoolteacher who has recently been widowed. The one long letter, addressed to her old friend, is a record of her emotional struggle for survival after her husband's abrupt decision to take a second wife. Although sanctioned by Islam, she feels his action is a calculated betrayal of her and their life together. This story sheds light on West African Islamic culture in terms of religion and family dynamics.

Buchi Emecheta, *The Bride Price*

Set in Nigeria in the late 1950s, this is the story of a fifteen-year-old girl, who after her father dies, goes to live in a small town where traditions are strong. With no sisters, a very young brother, and a mother who is too busy with her new life to pay much attention or give her advice, only the schoolteacher offers kindness and gentleness to this girl who falls in love with the son of a slave. This story offers insights into Nigerian culture, such as sexual taboos, funerals, voodoo, tribal beliefs mixed with Christianity, forced marriage and sex, and paying bride prices.

Fadia Faqir, *Pillars of Salt*

This is the story of two women, Maha, a Bedouin from the Jordan Valley who marries the love of her life, and yet which does not save her from repression and violence; and Um Saad, a woman from Amman who is in love with a Cicassian, but who has been married off to an older man. She must yield to the humiliation of his bringing home a new, young wife. Both women have been confined to a mental hospital in Jordan during and after the British mandate. They find themselves sharing a room, and after the initial tension, they become friends and begin sharing their life stories. The storyteller, an outsider, interlaces the narratives much like in the tradition of the *Arabian Nights*, telling this story during Ramadan. Relying on both Muslim and Christian theological sources, it reveals the struggle of Arab women to survive in a male-dominated society.

Carolina Maria de Jesus, *Child of the Dark*

Written on scraps of paper picked from gutters, this is the journal written from 1955–1960 that chronicles the true life of a street scavenger, Carolina Maria de Jesus, who fought daily for survival of herself and her three illegitimate children in a Brazilian favela, a human garbage dump, home of the poor, the hungry, and the desperate; a place where there is open and free sex, prostitution, violence and drunkenness. Carolina makes the comment that the rich despise poverty, and that the favela has been "discarded" by the politicians. She also has a hard time believing in God, though she tells the gypsies who camp in the favela, and who dump their excrement in the streets, that God will come and fix everything in the world, that Jesus will come to earth and judge the good and the bad! Her personal diary sheds light on the sordid plight of slum dwellers around the world.

Sahar Khalifeh, *Wild Thorns*

This compelling novel offers insights into the unspoken feelings of Palestinians, and their determination to survive. This is the story of Usama, a young Palestinian who has just returned from the Gulf, where he has been working as a translator. A supporter of the resistance movement, he has come home to the Israeli-occupied West Bank on a mission: to blow up the buses that transport Palestinian workers into Israel everyday. However, he is shocked to learn that many of his fellow citizens have adjusted to life under military rule. Hurt by harsh exchanges between friends and family, and with his mind torn, he sets out to accomplish his mission anyway. This book offers unsentimental portrayals of everyday life and personal relations under the occupation.

Sindiwe Magona, *Mother to Mother*

In 1993 Amy Biehl was killed by a mob of black youth in Guguletu, South Africa. Amy, a white American, had gone to South Africa to help black people prepare for the country's first truly democratic elections. Ironically, those who killed her were precisely the people for whom she held a huge compassion, understanding what they had suffered. While much was heard about the victim and her life, nothing was said about the world of her killers, the legacy of apartheid, and an environment that failed to nurture them in the higher ideals of humanity. Raised in a system that bred senseless inter- and intra-racial violence that promoted a twisted sense of right and wrong, this is a gripping novel in which the killer's mother, grief-stricken, dredges up memories of her own girlhood, her mother's monthly examinations of her virginity, her exile to a far away village, her pregnancy, her being forced to leave school and marry the boy who had betrayed her, and the economic and political environment in which she had to raise her only son. In looking for answers herself, and imagining the other mother's pain, she draws a portrait of her son and his world.

J. Nozipo Maraire, *Zenzele: A Letter for My Daughter*

This novel is written as a letter from a Zimbabwean mother to her daughter, a student at Harvard, who has rejected tradition and heritage for the freedom and opportunity of the western culture. This is an interweaving of history and memories in the tradition of the village storyteller by a mother who bares her soul and a past that parallels Zimbabwe's struggle for independence. Its themes are conflict, principle, prejudice, love, and transcendence.

Kamala Markandaya, *Nectar in a Sieve*

This is about a simple peasant woman from a primitive village in India, named Rukmani, who recounts her story in the twilight of her years, knowing that death is imminent. Married as a child bride at age twelve without dowry to a tenant farmer she had never seen, but who showed her love, and having to leave her own family, she worked beside her husband, fighting both poverty and disaster. She watched as one baby died from starvation, as her only daughter and first-born child became a prostitute, and as her sons left the land for jobs that she distrusted. What she had wanted was food, shelter, and happiness, but in the end it was all taken from her. Sorrow following sorrow, she continued on, confronting the issues of daily life. It is the story of thousands of women in India.

Farnoosh Moshiri, *The Bathhouse*

This intense emotional story begins with the arrest of a seventeen-year-old girl in the early days of the fundamentalist revolution in Iran when the Ayatollah took over in 1979. Imprisoned because of her brother's leftist politics, she is placed in a makeshift jail, a former bathhouse, along with other women. Based on interviews with several Iranian women who had been imprisoned in such a place, this story includes televised "confessions" of repentants, stoning of accused "lesbians," and the death of prisoners by execution. It documents not only their torment, but also their courage and humanity in the face of tyrants.

Queen Noor, *Leap of Faith: Memoirs of an Unexpected Life*[8]

This is Lisa Halaby's own remarkable story of how she won the heart of King Hussein of Jordan, and lost her heart to his people. She weaves into their own personal love story, the story of the Arab quest for peace, as well as King Hussein's efforts to bring peace to the region, the setbacks of the Gulf War, and the assassination of Prime Minister Rabin of Israel. She

8. Having traveled over the years throughout Jordan with my husband who is an archaeologist and professor of ancient history, and because he had been instrumental in connecting the Assistant Director of the Department of Antiquities up with the museum curator at the Cincinnati Art Museum, we were invited to dine with Queen Noor when she visited the United States in 1994 to dedicate a piece of Nabatean art, a statue of Tyche crowned with a Zodiac, and to dedicate the opening of a mosque in Cincinnati. It was quite an experience and an honor!

offers an insider's explanation into the rift between the Israelis, the Arabs, and the United States. It's a history lesson woven into a love story, and a love story woven against a political backdrop of the Middle East.

Patricia Powell, *Me Dying Trial*

Set in Jamaica, this story introduces Gwennie Glaspole, a schoolteacher trapped in an unhappy abusive marriage with five children, whose escape into the arms of another man brings about the birth of her sixth child and fiercely independent daughter, Peppy. Gwennie resists Jamaican cultural expectations of playing dutiful wife and mother. Instead, she dreams of making a new and better life in America. Finally she moves to Connecticut, and is able to eventually send for her children. It is a story about church, religious values, community, extended family, and economics. It's about living by trial and error.

Nawal El Saadawi, *Woman at Point Zero*

Being interviewed from her prison cell, Firdaus, who has been sentenced to die, and who was executed in 1974 for killing a pimp in a Cairo street, tells the true story of her life from village childhood to city prostitute. Born into the Egyptian lower class, with no rights, watched closely by both men and women, this is a story about what it means to live honorably, and die free. According to Saadawi, women in Egypt are seen as either virgins or whores, defined as such by a political system of males who themselves have no honor. She is advocating that men and their political systems must change if the fate of women is to ever change in Egypt. Saadawi is an Egyptian feminist, socialist, medical doctor, and writer. Also read *The Innocence of the Devil*, another novel in which she powerfully confronts the role of women in Muslim society, again questioning the religious as well as the secular foundations of patriarchal authority.

Hanan al-Shaykh, *Women of Sand and Myrrh*

This is the story of four women, living in an unnamed Arab desert state rich with oil, who are struggling to cope in a society where they are treated to every luxury but freedom. Suha is a Lebanese woman with a French European cultural background, trying to adjust to the Arab desert culture; Tamr is a woman from a Bedouin culture trying to make it after two bad marriages; Suzanne is a housewife from Texas whose husband, an oil businessman, leaves her lonely for love; and Nur is a filthy rich child of an oil sheik, who has lived a completely perverted and corrupt life. Their life stories weave together a rich tapestry of themes of religion, sex, marriage, housekeeping, and friendship as they really are in the golden cage of the Gulf region. Also read *I Sweep the Sun off Rooftops*, a collection of seventeen short stories that reflect the relationships that shape the Arab landscape, from a woman who feigns insanity to escape an empty marriage, to a young Dutch missionary who gets slowly drawn into the world of the Yemini village where she has been sent to work, to another woman whose lighthearted attempt at contacting the dead leads her to the spirit of her deceased husband.

Xinran, *The Good Women of China*

These are a collection of true stories that poured forth from anonymous women in attempts at self-understanding in a painfully restricted society before Deng Xiaoping's efforts to "open up" and "reform" China in the late 1980s. The stories told had taken place all over the country, at different times over the past seven or so decades, and came from women of very different social, cultural, and professional backgrounds. They revealed secret personal as well as political worlds that had been hidden from view. They talk about family and child issues, marriage, education, the communist revolution and the Cultural Revolution. Finally, it is a study on the condition of women in China. To me they represent stories of an extended time living in a country that forbid any practice of religion. While the author would have risked going to prison for writing such a book in China, in England it became possible.

5

Recommendations for Starting and Running a Christian Reader's Group

REALIZING WHAT your talents are, and then trying to find a way to use them to serve is sometimes difficult. Finding myself in a church where men do most of the primary ministering, and having absolutely no musical talents and very little appreciation for watching babies or working with small children, I was left wondering what a girl like me could possibly contribute. One Sunday our minister, Phil LeMaster, preached a sermon challenging members of the congregation to find the thing God has given them a passion to do and use it to serve the church. After the sermon ended, our elders sent around a lengthy form listing all the areas in the church for which workers were needed. Many of them would have been perfectly pleasant duties to perform, while others would have sent me running for the door. Thankfully, God did not create us to be exactly alike! Once everyone got a copy of the list, Phil added that if anyone had a desire to do anything that was not on the list to write it in and the minister of involvement would consider it. Right away I wrote down the only two things I truly love in this world as far as work is concerned, and that is reading and writing. I volunteered to begin either a book club or a writer's group. A few days later I received a phone call asking me about the book club idea. Once I explained my vision, I was asked to write up a proposal for the elders. The rest is history! It has truly been one of the most enjoyable things I have ever done, and I highly recommend anyone who loves to read to consider starting one herself! I hope the following suggestions can be of help.

1. Have a vision, and set your goals.

Before you even get started, decide what you want the focus, or the goal, of your group to be. Before our group got started, I knew that I wanted to open it up to anybody in our town, or anybody in the county for that matter, who would be interested in reading Christian fiction. Even though our church was going to sponsor the reading group, I envisioned it being an outreach to include others not in our particular congregation. To this end we decided to advertise our reader's group in the local newspaper, as well as on the local radio station. As a result, we started with women from several different denominations. On occasion we have even had women who did not consider themselves to be Christian attend the group because of the book titles we were reading. The ripple effect of our reading group has spread even wider across the boundaries of not only our town, but of our state, to friends and relatives (mothers, sisters, daughters, and even husbands) of members of our group, as well as others who keep informed on our book selections and read even though they do not come to the discussion group. Our church secretary says that sales people have dropped by and seen the books sitting around her office, and have inquired about them. A police officer that gives driving tests from the church parking lot has read many of the books after having found out that we were reading Christian fiction.

This has been the most exciting part of running a book club devoted to reading Christian fiction. There are so many people out there who want to read, and are especially interested in reading something that is not only wholesome and entertaining, but that will challenge their spirits as well! However, other book clubs have different focuses than ours, which is bringing together different women from different denominations, as well as reaching women who do not attend church anywhere, but who like to read. You may want to start a book club with just a few women that you know who love to read. Or, you may want to start one just for women in your own church congregation. There are reader's groups that focus on mothers with their daughters, designed particularly to encourage communication and a shared activity between moms and daughters. The youth minister in our church wants to start up a reader's group to encourage the teens in our community to read and discuss Christian fiction. Someone asked me at a workshop if men ever attend reader's groups. Historically book groups have predominately been made up of women. However, there are plenty of men who like to read fiction, and there are sometimes mixed groups, but typically that is not the case. Men have been invited (though rather informally) to our group, though none have ever come. What I do know, though, is that some of the men in our church are reading some of the books! Even our minister has said on occasion that he would like to be in on the discussion of a particular book, but he thought that if he showed up to the meeting no one would talk. We have all had a good laugh over that, because most of us would never be able to keep quiet even if he were running the whole show!

I would like to make one final comment here in regards to the size of a reading group. I have had women ask me what the best size is for having book discussions. In my own experience, when we have had anywhere from eight to fifteen women we could still have great discussions. When we have gotten up to around twenty plus women because they heard we were going to discuss a particular book (one instance was when we returned from a summer break and were going to discuss Jan Karon's *At Home in Mitford*, which was a very popular book!), there was still discussion, though it ended up being carried on by only a few of the women who always have something to say anyway! But that was still one of my most delightful experiences! Since then I have only asked the group on one occasion to stop inviting any more of their friends, since we were about to burst out of our room, and were losing the small amount of intimacy that we still had. I would finally suggest that you do whatever feels best and works best for your individual group, but do consider size when creating your vision of what you want your group to be.

2. Set a time and a place.

Once you have met with members of your book group for the first time, it would be a good idea to ask everyone what would be the best time for them to meet, and then stick to that from then on. Our group picked the second Tuesday evening of every month from 7:00 to 8:00. You probably would want to avoid Wednesday nights since most churches have bible studies on that night. My only other suggestion would be to check on other group meetings in your area, or in your church in order to make sure that there are no other conflicts. Of course, there may always be something going on every night of the month, but you must finally commit to something. And, depending on your group, you might even consider meeting during the daytime. Also, one final note: most book groups meet only once a month. However, it is up to your group if you want to read more often than that. Remember, it is your group!

In terms of where to meet, my number one suggestion is to meet somewhere conducive to book discussions. We started out in the chapel room of our church since it was a smaller sized room. We moved the chairs around a coffee table in a big circle, but afterwards we all decided we didn't like that because of the discomfort we felt not having our legs hidden under a table, and having nothing to put our arms and elbows on!

It wasn't until our third month that we settled into the library room where there is one long table with chairs that we can all sit around. Sometimes we have not been able to get everyone around the table and we have had to sit on a pew located along one wall, but that is still where we are happiest, and where we have stayed. (I would just like to note that even though we changed rooms three times before we were comfortably settled in, we were always in the church building, and new members could always find us.)

If you do not want to meet with your reader's group in a church building, or are unable to, there are usually locations around town that are designed for community groups to use. Bank buildings often have community rooms, so do city libraries, and so do some bookstores. Also, coffee shops often allow groups to meet in them, especially if group members buy their drinks there. And one other type of place to consider meeting in is your favorite restaurant! In any case, all you have to do is pick up the phone and check around. Finally, many book groups meet in private homes. However, you may only want to do this if you know all the members. One member may volunteer her home for every meeting, or you may want to meet in a different member's home each month.

One final note about where you meet. When making this decision, you may want to consider whether or not you want to serve snacks. When our group started, I was so eager for everyone to be happy that I asked to have included in the church budget for our book club enough money to feed an army! When we started as a group we were enjoying cheese balls, and meat trays, and chips and dips, and sweets, as well as a whole assortment of drinks; and we did this for about a year. Eventually I noticed that quite a bit of the food was being left over. Not that the ministers and ladies who came into the church to work the next day minded, but I began to realize that the women in our group were indeed coming because they liked the good discussions we were having, and it had nothing to do with the food at all! Now we just serve drinks and some type of cookies or holiday candy (and my favorites are Halloween, Valentine's Day, and Easter!). Always we have coffee and at least two types of sodas, including something without caffeine. Still the candy or cookies are very rarely touched, yet I just can't bring myself to stop serving it. I guess I would feel like I was being too inhospitable. Anyway, it does all look good sitting on the table! Now, we have had some specific party occasions when we've planned that no one will eat before the book club meeting. For example, we had a rather large Christmas party one year, when every member brought her favorite finger food, and the church provided the drinks. That year we cut our book discussion time in half, even though everyone ended up staying almost twice the amount of time!

Wherever you decide to meet, you will finally have to give the issue of whether or not to serve food and/or drinks some thought. What that means is that you must have a place to serve them, and access to plates, cups, napkins, and whatever else you might need. Fortunately the library room in our church where we meet has a built-in counter, a sink, and a small refrigerator. Since the church sponsors our reader's group, they have written the expenses for it into their budget. If that is not going to be the case for your group, then you might want to ask everyone to contribute something each meeting, or else have one different person take care of everything each month so that every member has a chance to play hostess. If you meet in a coffee shop or restaurant somewhere, the entire problem becomes moot, and the only consideration to make would be to the establishment itself, and in making sure that most of the women at least make some kind of food or drink purchase out of courtesy.

The only other issue involved in serving snacks, which is if you are not going to meet in a food establishment, is to consider when they will be served. We have ours out from the beginning so that everyone can get their drinks and food right away if they want them. I personally have no problem with people sipping their drinks and munching on food during the meeting, and I can't recall that anyone has ever had the poor manners to try to talk with their mouths full. However, another option would be to serve snacks after the meeting, so that you can extend your time of fellowship. Again, I would say that it all goes back to the vision and goals you have for your own group.

3. Find members who will be committed to reading!

It is not that difficult to start a book club. However, to keep one running you must have people who are committed to reading all of the books. This may sound like an obvious suggestion, but I put it in here because based on my experience you might have some women who are primarily looking for another opportunity to socialize, or who just sometimes like to read, or who only like certain types of stories, and won't read anything else. Now depending on the focus of your group, you may let some of these women in, but you better not let the majority of them be picky types or non-readers. This is why I suggest that you consider choosing a few challenging books the first couple of months. Women who only like to read what I call

Christian pulp fiction may not have ever tried the more literary works, and thus may find out that they really are wonderful stories, and that they have been missing out on these books for far too long! However, if they don't like the books, you will be left with a core group of women who are indeed far more serious readers and who will probably enjoy dissecting the works during an hour-long book club discussion. In either case, this should help alleviate the problem by causing a few "readers" to drop by the wayside early on. Certainly there are reasons why someone may not be able to read a particular month's selection, but if this keeps happening, you will find that your discussions may be all but nonexistent.

And this leads me to my other point. You may want to ask your club members to commit to participating, at least as much as they feel comfortable, in the book discussions. This area is a little bit trickier, primarily because of all the different personality types. Some women may start out shy, but may loosen up as the months go by. Some women may only talk when they feel that another person is not dominating the discussion. Others may only talk whenever there is so much excitement that it seems everyone is trying to get in a word. Whatever the case may be, you may want to insure at the beginning that you get at least some women who know that they want to talk about the books within a group setting.

The only other commitments, or rules you may want the group members to keep are to listen when others are speaking, which involves basic common courtesy, and to be polite at all times. And I strongly urge that if you have a reader's group with women or men from various Christian backgrounds, that you consider avoiding reading books that contain any controversial theological content that could invite dissension among the group, and that you likewise discourage any negative comments regarding any religious group or denomination. I suggest making it clear from the start that everyone agree to respect all other members' religious differences, and that your book club not be a place to try to convert others over to your beliefs.

4. Decide on what your group will read.

Before we even started our reader's group, I made a commitment to variety! My vision was to first of all stretch everyone's reading beyond the comfort zone of pulp fiction. This meant that I wanted to include on the reading list some literary classics, both Christian and non-Christian. Secondly, I made the decision that we would not read more than one book by an author within a year's time. And thirdly, I wanted to vary the genre every month within a year so that the reading list would not only try to meet everyone's personal tastes, but that it might stretch everyone's entire reading experience! I feel it is to this end that we have in part succeeded as a group.

Even though not every lady has like every book that we have read every single month, every member knows that the next month's book selection will be something entirely different, and thus continually look forward with hopefulness and excitement. Some women have even remarked that they did not expect to like a certain book, like *A Requiem for Love* by Calvin Miller, for example, but after having read it because of the book club, they suddenly had a new favorite book that they could recommend to their friends and family members who were avid readers! One woman in particular bought several copies of that book alone to send out as Christmas presents that year. This same thing has happened with several others of the books as well. My suggestion would be to not be afraid to make some choices that you might consider as rather unusual, or even works that you think people might not prefer, when making up your reading list. Be adventurous, and you might just be surprised! When I chose Nathaniel Hawthorne's American classic, *The Scarlet Letter*, I got this overwhelming, "Oh, No! I had to read that in high school!" from most women in the group. However, I stuck to my guns by explaining to them that I did not believe Hawthorne ever expected young teenagers to be his audience for that work. I am very happy to say that we had one of our most animated book discussions ever over the themes running through *The Scarlet Letter*, and that those same women who balked at having to read it came back and said that they got far more out of it than they ever did when they read it as a young person!

Other works that I have included on the reading list are some non-fiction titles such as *The Hiding Place* and *Tuesdays With Morrie*. I included these because first of all, *The Hiding Place*, which is an autobiographical work, is a Christian classic, and I personally believe that everyone can benefit spiritually from reading it, and secondly because a book like *Tuesdays With Morrie*, which is more of a memoir, hit *The New York Times* bestseller list, as well as Oprah's book club list, and thus not only was it timely to read, but the subject matter was extremely appropriate for a Christian reader's group discussion! Another book that was an Oprah selection was Barbara Kingsolver's *The Poisonwood Bible*, which had also been on *The NY Times* bestseller list. It just so happened that I chose it as our group's summer reading selection a month before Oprah did, which didn't go over as well with the group as the summer before when I had left them off with the first book in the Mitford series. I think everyone was hoping for more light-hearted, entertaining reading over the summer, but I just saw it as a really good book that had more pages in it than what I would normally ask people to read during the rest of the year. However, as soon as Oprah made it her book club selection, it suddenly changed how everyone viewed having to read it! That became yet another time when I felt grateful for Oprah's influence on America's reading! I would also like to add here a note concerning the discussion we were blessed to have concerning *The Poisonwood Bible*. One woman who comes to our group on occasion had been a missionary in that part of Africa during the time of the setting of that novel, and was very willing to share and compare her experiences with those of the main characters. She said that she had not been so moved by a work of fiction, as she was by that story in a very long time! Again, just another reason to check out books on the bestseller lists every now and then.

The other advice I would offer someone who is trying to make up a working syllabus for the year would be to not only consider variety, but to consider holidays when certain books or themes running through books might be appropriate. These can include not only Christmas, which is a great time to read a holiday story, but consider Valentine's Day in February, Mother's Day in May, possibly Halloween in October and Thanksgiving in November, as well as all the seasons of spring, summer, fall, and winter. I wouldn't say that you always have to be so thematic, and you can tell by my own book club syllabi that I haven't, though I have consistently chosen Christmas stories in December and "love" stories in February, and one year in October I even selected for our group Edgar Lee Masters' literary classic, *Spoon River Anthology*, since I thought that reading epitaphs of dead people for a story would be appropriate right before Halloween!

Another situation in which you might want to allow for some flexibility in your syllabus is if you ever find yourself fortunate enough, because of where you live, to have a published author come visit your town! Here in this very small Eastern Kentucky town, which might seem like an unlikely place for an author to visit, sits the campus of a Christian college which sponsors, every year in March, a Ladies' Day weekend. When we were so blessed to have Liz Curtis Higgs come in as the main speaker, our book club read as that month's selection *Bookends*, which is one of her fictional works. Believe me, that certainly added an extra dimension of excitement to our club!

My final suggestions are these: That you decide up front whether or not you want to make up your syllabus one year at a time, or month by month; that you decide how many months during the year you want to meet; and that you decide who will be responsible for making the decisions as to the book titles that you will read. First of all, if you make the syllabus up one year at a time, everyone will know what it is you will be reading, and you won't have to worry about it but once a year. However, month by month allows not only for the element of surprise, but for the most flexibility in case there is a hot new release, or a book hits the bestseller list that you know your group would want to read, or just in the case of some other unforeseen event. Whichever method you choose though, keep in mind that most people like to be up on the latest and the best of books that hit the market, and you don't want your reader's feeling left behind.

Also when you make up a syllabus you need to have some idea as to whether your group will want to meet all year round, or if they will want to take some summer months off. So far our group has always only met for nine months during each year, though I know that almost everyone, though they want some summer months off, would prefer only taking off two instead of three. However, since I am married to a professor of ancient history and archaeology, who not only goes on summer digs, but who also takes students on summer study tours to the Middle East, and because I always want to join him, we have yet to meet during the months of June, July, or August. Fortunately, these are heavy vacation months for almost everyone, and so even though there is some grumbling and regret about taking three months off, everyone has thus far eagerly returned in the fall! During the summer though, I have either left everyone with a book in a series (so that if they like it they can read the entire series over the summer), or else I have picked a thicker book than what I would have otherwise chosen during the rest of the year. Taking all this time off during the summer also affords me the time to catch up on a lot of reading myself, especially since I try to read everything in advance of bringing it into the book club. But however you choose to do things, readers will continue to read during the summer months, and all that will be lost to anyone will be the great discussions that they all could have had!

And finally, you will have to make a decision as to who will choose the books that your club will read. In the case of our book club, I have thus far picked all the books. However, there are several options as to how this could be handled. One way is that a different person could be in charge of choosing the book each month, though this is typically not how it is done. Another option is to let the entire group help make the decisions, a method which would work better if you made up your syllabus a year at a time. Also, you could just involve a couple of people in the decision-making process, but I would suggest doing it this way only as long as everyone in the group feels good about who is doing it, and no one ends up feeling excluded. However, sometimes anarchy works best, and that way there is only one person to be upset with if things aren't going well. I always stay open to suggestions, and have several books that have been recommended to me on my list of titles to read in the near future. The only Christian titles that I deliberately exclude are ones that I feel might cause even the slightest bit of dissension due to arguable theology, or are already very well known to the majority of Christian fiction readers, or are part of a very lengthy series.

5. Decide on how you would like your group members to purchase their books.

There are several avenues for ensuring that your reader's group members get their books. Probably one of the most common is to ask your local Christian bookstore, or any bookstore for that matter, to purchase them for you each month. Most bookstores are more than happy to accommodate local book clubs, as this helps their business. Most chain bookstores order such a large variety of both Christian and non-Christian titles that they would have no problem in ordering any book your club might be interested in reading. While I was finishing writing my Master's thesis I worked in a small local bookstore in Oxford, Ohio. I remember that we ordered books for several book clubs that existed in that town. Someone from the club would be responsible for calling in the order, and when the books came in we would just hold them behind the counter until the women came in to purchase their copies. The only consideration you should try to make to the bookstore when ordering this way is that you not request more books to be ordered than what you are going to need for your group, unless the manager states up front that sending books back to their distributors or putting extra books on their shelves would not be a problem.

Another way to handle this concern is to make every member responsible for acquiring her own copy of the book club's selection every month, though this would be easier if you lived in a large enough town where there were several bookstores. Since most bookstores don't keep more than a single copy of any one title on their shelves, or even in stock for that matter, in an area where there may be only one or two stores, you might end up with several women having to request, possibly at all different times throughout any given month, that the bookstore special order her a copy of the books, and this could quickly become tiresome for all parties concerned. However, with modern technology, this problem could be easily solved if everyone had access to the Internet. Books are extremely easy to purchase on-line, and I have included in Appendix A a whole host of web site addresses for ordering books. All anyone needs to be able to purchase books on-line is a credit card number, and then you can usually receive your book orders at your home within one week. I have been doing this for years, and I highly recommend it!

This leads me to how your book club can order their books if you are church sponsored. In this case, the church can not only agree to purchase up front every month all the books that your club will need, but may consider absorbing the cost for any book that does not sell right away. Every month, after I have selected the book title, the church's secretary, with access to a credit card, either calls in the purchase to Christian Book Distributors (CBD), or else orders them on-line after I have found the lowest purchase price available. Doing it this way enables us to have, sitting on the table in the room where we meet at the beginning of every book club meeting, the next month's selection ready for purchase. Our church secretary comes to all of our book club meetings and has taken responsibility for selling the books to each of the ladies, who pay her either by cash, or else by writing out a check made payable to the church. The money from the sale of the books then goes back into the church's account. So far, whenever we have ordered more books than we have needed for the book club members, we have either advertised to our own church members that we have extra copies available for sale in the church office, or sometimes the church has given away copies to people who could not afford them, or else they have eventually been sold to people who have wandered into the church office for various reasons and have seen them sitting on the shelves. The opposite problem comes whenever we have not ordered enough copies of any given book to meet the requests of people who would like to purchase a particular title due to its enormous popularity (which is something very hard to predict), usually spread by word of mouth! In these cases we try to encourage whoever is making the request to purchase their own copy through a bookstore, or else borrow a copy from a friend, or if those avenues both fail, to wait until after the reader's group meets, and then check the book out of the church's library, where one copy always ends up. In any event, not putting some kind of control on your group's membership size can make purchasing books for your club a guessing game at best.

6. Consider how you will organize your group leadership.

If you know anything about group dynamics, then you know that no matter what kind of group you are putting together, it will always run more smoothly when someone is in charge! Likewise, so too can a book discussion group benefit by having a leader. Some book groups around the country call in a professional leader, but those folks have to be paid, and they usually charge anywhere from $10 to $15 or more, depending on where you live, per person per meeting, and most of the time require a ten month payment in advance. However, a huge number of book groups run things themselves internally. But whichever route you decide to take, having an appointed or designated leader will definitely provide better structure, and it is to that end that I will offer up some advice on the subject.

First of all, I would suggest that you openly discuss and set guidelines and expectations for what you want your leader to do, and then determine if you want to appoint one individual to lead for a year, or if you want to change the group leader month-to-month. However, I would like to make one small note: if *every* group member commits to participating equally and freely, the group will probably run more smoothly.

No matter what the title designation is, whether it be leader, organizer, or facilitator, there are a few things this person should commit to doing, and being negligent in any one of these details could corrode an otherwise good reading group. Number one, she should make sure the meeting starts and ends at the appointed time, so that your meetings do not drag on past the hour or so that each member has committed to. Remember, everyone's time is precious, and it would be discourteous to be neglectful of this. If your group's discussion gets too far off track, or if everyone starts talking at once, or if someone monopolizes the conversation, your group leader should devise a plan for correcting these problems. Also, someone could do some preparation and research on the book before the meeting, maybe prepare some biographical material on the author, bring in applicable biblical references, any pictures or poems that the author may refer to, or bring in any supplemental material or feature stories on the author, or reviews on the book. And finally, someone, or everyone could even develop a few questions to start the discussion.

By virtue of my education and my background, I have been able to provide not only discussion questions for our reader's group, but I have been able to provide many outside resources and research as well. For example, when we read Liz Curtis Higgs' *Bookends*, I brought in a one-page handout on the Moravians (put together with the help of my husband who teaches a course in church history). I also searched on the Internet and found a two-page interview with her, which I also photocopied and brought in for everyone. When we read *The Believers*, by Janice Holt Giles, I brought in a tourist brochure for everyone on the Historic Shaker Village of Pleasant Hill, located in Kentucky, which had nice color photos, a map on how to get there, and some of the history of the Shakers. When we read Jan Karon's *At Home in Mitford* I brought in all kinds of goodies that Viking/Penguin Press had put out for marketing purposes, like a Mitford bookmark, a seventeen-page readers guide to the entire series, copies of her newsletters, plus a Father Tim's sermon keepsake for every member, which I found at Joseph Beth Bookstore in Lexington, Kentucky. When we read *The Scarlet Letter* I provided historical information concerning the Puritans, and when we read *A Skeleton in God's Closet*, I was able to provide a little bit of not so well known information as to why he wanted to write a book with such a theme: Maier had felt that someday somebody might want to pull such an elaborate and believable hoax as the one described, and he wanted to pre-empt it with a fictional account, hoping that readers would remember that they had read about archaeologists digging up the bones of Jesus in a novel. When we read *Tuesdays With Morrie*, one of the television networks had just aired a made for TV movie. I was able to obtain the videotape, and brought it in for our group members to take home and view. These are all examples of ways that I have tried to bring in outside resources into our book club, and though you probably will not always be able to provide such neat stuff, it can be done more often than you might think, and it always adds to the group's enthusiasm for the book you are discussing!

Another thing that a group leader can do is set the tone of the discussion. They may be casual/conversational, structured/academic, or intense/emotional, and it might not only have to do with the personalities of the people in your group, but also with your group leader's personality. Most groups, according to research, say that their discussions are casual/conversational, though oftentimes serious, yet they still remain fun, humorous, as well as on occasion intensely emotional. Whew! I am happy to report that ours is all of that too, though maybe not every single month, depending on the book we are discussing! But no matter what, they are always friendly, respectful, and safe. In the end, whoever leads your group, should lead it according to the group's personality and desires. If the group wants a lecture, then so be it (ours has turned into one maybe twice in three years). If the group doesn't want to pick every little thing in the book apart, then so be it. If the group doesn't want to discuss the author's intentions, and wants to discuss the work only on a personal level, then so be it. And finally, be open to the fact that anyone in your group could emerge as your leader. If she enjoys it and is good at it, open your arms to her in appreciation!

7. Decide on what you will discuss during your book club meetings.

The safest way to handle any book club discussion is to have at least some questions ready made, either to get things rolling, or to help when there is a lull. As I mentioned before, as a group you can decide on who will be responsible for writing questions for your book discussions. It might be one person who is particularly good at it and who enjoys it, or it might be that you will want everyone in the group to be active readers and come to your meetings with at least one or two questions apiece. Also, as I mentioned previously concerning the tone and atmosphere of your club, it may take a little time for your group to get a feel for within what type of framework your discussions will take place. What I mean by this is that your group may want things to be completely relaxed, to be a break from their everyday stress, and therefore may only want to talk about the characters, who they liked and who they didn't and why, and what they thought about the ending, and who would play what parts in the movie version. Or, your group may prefer things to be more academic than that, meaning that as long as they put forth the effort to read a particular book, they will prefer that the book club be a forum where they dig into the text more in order that they get the most out of it. In other words, they may want the book club to be a place where they come to learn, and that it should not take on the framework of being just another social meeting. Then, you may have a group who prefers far more emotionally intense discussions, and therefore they may want to get into more passionate, as well as intellectual, discussions. That is, they will want to dig into the soul of every book as much as possible. Now, what may really happen is that you will have a combination of these types in your group, and depending on how it is organized, you may have a version of any one of these depending on the work being discussed, and/or the overall mood of the group during any given month. Hopefully though, however diverse the level of discourse may be among your group members, you will be able to find a level of compromise that will enable you to satisfy everyone's personalities. I have to admit that I personally am more academic in my approach to works of fiction, mixed up with a strong desire as well to lay bare the soul of every work (thus my passion to earn degrees in the study of literature)! However, I recognize that not everyone feels or thinks the way I do, and so I try to write a combination of questions that will suite a variety of tastes, minus, as you can observe, any questions on who might play what character in a movie version of a book! (In fact, I would prefer it if no one in my group knew I had even thought of such a thing! Ha!) More seriously though, I need mention here that I hold a particular philosophy as to what I want a Christian reader's group to be, and that is, as I have already stated, a place to promote spiritual growth. I personally hold the belief that a book club should enrich and challenge individuals to that end, and that people can read purely for pleasure on their own. However, since it is very difficult to determine where someone else is in their own spiritual walk, I have brought into the club books that center around characters and their actions, and have found that sometimes humor and frivolity can be excellent spiritual medicine!

So besides designing questions that have to do with characters and the storyline, what else can you talk about? I have included discussion guides to thirty-four different works that address questions concerning characters' actions, personality traits, development, interaction with others as well as their own situations; religious or social implications of the story, and this would include any relevant biblical passages that would help to shed light on anything concerning the story; points of conflict and resolution; credibility; the work's similarities to other works; narrative style and technique; theme; point of view; setting; reader's own personal response; and personal reference. For definitions of some of these terms, as well as other literary terms that could further aid in book discussions, see Appendix B.

I include the discussion guides, not only so that you may use them as they are written, but so you may use them as models of to how to write your own questions for books that I have not included. I would like to make a few suggestions as to how to use questions, whether mine or your own. First of all, if one person is in charge of making up the questions, don't distribute them in advance of the book club meeting. Doing so might affect the way each person reads the works, and what she might bring to a text without any outside influences while she is reading. Also, it might feel to everyone that they have to be able to answer the questions, much like a test, and that they are students and the discussion leader is the teacher, which is a situation you want to try to avoid. Also, if one person is in charge of making the questions, someone might want to photocopy enough for everyone in the group so that each member has access to them and can look them over before the meeting begins. I do this for my group, and it works well on two levels. One, they get a chance to refresh their memories as to different aspects and details of the story, and two, they get a chance to see where I am going with the line of questioning. However, I never stick strictly to my questions. I always begin every meeting by opening discussion to anyone who wants to go first concerning any topic, though it usually takes the form of, "Did you like this book or not, and why or why not?" or, "What did you like most or least about this book?" Most of the time that gets the ball rolling, and then the discussion progresses from there, with members using the questions as springboards to discussing what interests them the most. It is only when no one speaks up, or when there is a lull in the discussion, or when someone gets off track that I use the questions to bring them back to a discussion of the book, or just to get discussion moving along once again. Again, this needs to be part of the job of a discussion facilitator. I try not to control the discussion itself, but to keep it on the book so that our book club does not become just another social meeting. Over and over I have asked the women in our group if they would like for me to stop writing up the questions, and always the response has been a resounding "No." However, these question sheets are just what I have labeled them; they are "guides" and nothing more.

I want to add something here about allowing for personal responses and/or personal references to the books. Some books, more than others, invite various kinds of personal responses, meaning that sometimes you just have to relate a personal story in regards to something the book has triggered in you. What I suggest when this happens is to either go with the flow if everyone in your group seems okay with this, or else limit these kinds of responses to only a few minutes each, and then bring the discussion back onto the book itself. This could be a very touchy thing to do, but if everyone has agreed up front that for the most part the group will only discuss elements within the book itself, then most people in the group will be grateful that your discussion leader will not tolerate lengthy diversions by any one person. However, this should be done as graciously as possible so that no one ends up being offended. I would never want to lose a member because she felt she was not allowed to talk about anything personal. I don't think we have had a single meeting yet when someone, including me, hasn't felt the desire to share something on a personal level, and that has been part of the joy of our club. But I think that if, in the end, everyone keeps in mind the goal and vision for the book club, you can remember that each woman has come together with every other woman, in what might otherwise be an unlikely grouping of personalities, because of her love for reading.

A typical book club meeting.

6

Sample Syllabi and Discussion Guides

Sample Syllabus I

1. *The Hiding Place* by Corrie TenBoom

This is a story about Corrie and her sister Betsie who are both sent to the concentration camps for helping the Jews. It is about the glory of God and the courage of a quiet Christian spinster whose life was transformed. Themes include forgiveness, how God can use weakness, how to love your enemies, how to deal with difficult people, and what to do when evil wins.

2. *Hind's Feet on High Places* by Hannah Hurnard

This is the allegorical story of Much-Afraid and her spiritual journey through difficult places with her two companions, Sorrow and Suffering, as she overcomes her fears and passes through many dangers until she mounts at last to the High Places. There she gains a new name and returns to her valley of service, transformed by her union with the loving Shepherd.

3. *The Screwtape Letters* by C. S. Lewis

This is a collection of fiendish letters from Screwtape to his nephew, the young Tempter Wormwood, giving devilish advise on capturing the soul of his "patient" so that he will not be won over by "the Enemy," or God. This book offers great insight into the nature of mankind.

4. *In His Steps* by Charles Sheldon

This is the original WWJD story, which was published in 1897 as a sermon series. Church members are challenged by their minister, Rev. Henry

Maxwell, to join him in a pledge that for one year they will make no major decisions without first asking, "What would Jesus do?"

5. *A Requiem for Love* by Calvin Miller

The first release in the "Symphony Trilogy", this poetic story tells the tale of the creation of Adam and Eve in the Garden of Eden, displaying the power of love as the Creator offers the gift of choice to the created.

6. *At Home in Mitford* by Jan Karon

This first book in the five part Mitford Series introduces us to the charming village of Mitford, North Carolina and the lovable people who live there, including Father Tim, the bachelor rector, a boisterous dog, a boy who needs adopting, an attractive unmarried neighbor who writes children stories about her cat, and some great older citizens too!

7. *A Skeleton in God's Closet* by Paul Maier

Dr. Jonathon Weber, professor and Biblical scholar, is spending his sabbatical leave on an archaeological dig in Israel. But a spectacular find becomes a nightmare that could be the death of Christianity. Will a skeleton almost 2,000 years old shed new light on the life of Jesus, or plunge the world into darkness and chaos?

8. *The Scarlet Letter* by Nathaniel Hawthorne

This American classic story, set in an early New England colony, shows the terrible impact one single act of passion has on the lives of three members of the community: Hester Prynne, who has been branded an adulteress and must forever wear the scarlet "A", the tortured Reverend Dimmesdale, who keeps his secret until the bitter end, and the vengeful Roger Chillingworth, who drives Dimmesdale to madness. Themes are of adultery and hypocrisy.

9. *The Christmas Cross* by Max Lucado

A book with interactive features that help to illustrate how one man finds his way home for the holidays. After a fight with his wife Meg, a Chicago journalist finds himself in a small Texas town on Christmas eve, lonely and alone, until he takes a trip into his past that holds the key to his future.

Discussion Guide

The Hiding Place (The Story of Corrie Ten Boom)

ISBN 0-553-25669-6 ❧ Bantam Books
241 pages ❧ autobiography

1. In the Preface on page viii (and on p.15) Corrie states that "[T]his is what the past is for! Every experience God gives us, every person He puts in our lives is the perfect preparation for the future that only He can see." The preparation that we receive for a particular calling is not always the preparation that we might have thought we needed. In other words, we might think someone else would be far more qualified for the job for far more obvious reasons. What preparation did Corrie and Betsie receive for the job that they would later be involved in? How is it that God can use the most ordinary and most unlikely people to do His work? Cite examples from the Bible of when God called people to do jobs for which they did not feel qualified.

2. Situations like the concentration camps that were set up during WWII often cause Christians as well as those yet converted to ask the question that Lieutenant Rahms asked Corrie: "Why should Christians be allowed to suffer?" "What kind of God would have let that old man [Corrie's father] die here in Scheveningen?' (p. 163). What was Corrie's response to the Lieutenant who asked that question? How would you answer that question, especially in the face of such tremendous persecution?

3. Discuss the significance of the title *The Hiding Place*, both literally and figuratively. On page 23, when Corrie's father is reading from Psalms 119:105–114 ("Thou art my hiding place and my shield: I hope in Thy word . . ."), Corrie wonders to herself, "What kind of hiding place? What was there to hide from?" Later, both Betsie and Corrie say that "His [God's] Will is our hiding place" (p. 67 and 224). Explain what they meant.

4. What is Corrie's knowledge of the world, or the evil in the world, until the full-blown persecution of the Jews? How does her perspective change? Would your reaction to the evil of the Holocaust be more like Corrie's or more like Betsie's? Discuss the difference.

5. Throughout the story Corrie paints for us a picture of God. One image of God is revealed through Betsie's eyes after Corrie has her dream/vision (p. 62–63): " . . . if God has shown us bad times ahead, it's enough for me that He knows about them. That's why He sometimes shows us things, you know—to tell us that this too is in His hands." What are some of the ways in which God takes care of and provides for, as well as intervenes in the lives of Corrie and Betsie?

6. Like all Christians, Corrie has been raised with the belief that one should not lie. "I had known from childhood that the earth opened up and the heavens rained fire upon liars . . ." (p. 66). However, she tells her first conscious lie in response to whether or not they owned a radio. From this point on lying becomes an issue, especially in terms of saving lives. See also pages 71, 79, 90–91, 110, and 115. Discuss the question, "Is it ever all right to lie?"

7. Corrie tells the story of Karel, the love of her youth, in Chapter 3 (p. 30–45). Karel was betrothed to another woman, and Corrie's father, knowing the hurt that Corrie felt, tells her that "God loves Karel—even more than you do—and if you ask Him, He will give you His love for this man, a love nothing can prevent, nothing can destroy. Whenever we cannot love in the old, human way, God can give us the perfect way" (p. 44–45). Discuss what form God's love took in Corrie's life. What form did God's love take in others' lives?

8. Some of Betsie's final words to Corrie in the concentration camp before she dies is to tell people "what we have learned here. We must tell them that there is no pit so deep that He is not deeper still" (p. 217). Discuss some of the circumstances of the prison camp that became living proof to Corrie and Betsie that this statement was true.

9. As the Sherrills state in the Preface (p. vii), after hearing a man tell of his experiences in a Nazi concentration camp, and then hearing Corrie Ten Boom's story, the story was the same, but their responses were so different! How would you explain how Corrie could tell her story and still radiate love, peace, and joy? How might this story help you personally?

Discussion Guide

Hinds' Feet on High Places by Hannah Hurnard
ISBN 0-8423-1429-6 ✌ Living Books/Tyndale House Publishers
254 pages ✌ allegory

1. In Chapter One, the Shepherd asks Much-Afraid if she is willing to be changed completely (p. 24). She answers very earnestly, "Yes, I am," but really has no idea what she is so fully agreeing to. He tells her that she must become very vulnerable to pain (p. 25), and that if she would know love she must know pain too (p. 27). Discuss this concept not only in terms of loving humankind, but also in terms of loving God. That is, after all, what the "High Places" is referring to. We want to learn to love God, and to love others as we love ourselves, so how come this will involve pain?

2. In Chapter Four, the Shepherd tells Much-Afraid, "Humble yourself, and you will find that Love is spreading a carpet beneath your feet" (p. 56). This is in reference to the wildflowers that grow with such abundant beauty and sweetness, and yet go unnoticed, so happy to love even though one is not loved in return. Discuss the difference between humility and humiliation, which is the name of the valley where Much-Afraid is from. Also, discuss the meaning of the water-song (p. 59, &184–185).

3. In the second half of Chapter Four, the Shepherd gives Much-Afraid as her two guides Sorrow and Suffering (p. 66–67). Much-Afraid asks if she couldn't be given Joy and Peace as companions instead. Why must sorrow and suffering come before joy and peace? Are they necessary in order for us to learn love? How was it that she was able to learn to accept sorrow and suffering? Like Much-Afraid, most of us fear sorrow and suffering. Are they a form of humiliation, or bringing about humility? Explain the concept in Chapter Five of sorrow being greater after pride.

4. If God plants the Desire for Love (to get to the High Places) in our hearts, how does Satan use fear, pride, resentment, self-pity, and bitterness to destroy that desire? It may well be his number one goal! Are there other works of the flesh that could destroy that desire?

5. Since this is an allegorical work, discuss the concept put forth in Chapters Six and Seven when Much-Afraid must detour through

the desert, away from her heart's desire, and then walk along the shores of loneliness. This is the place where she builds her first altar and lays down her will. She learns the lesson of the furnace of fire, as well as the stories of the thrashed grain, the potter and clay, and of Acceptance-With-Joy! The Shepherd tells her that she will always be able to hear and recognize his voice, and that she must always obey, no matter if the path looks impossible or even crazy (p. 93).

6. Continuing in Chapters Seven, Eight, and Nine, there is more delay, and this is when her enemies seem their strongest. Why? What lessons is Much-Afraid learning during this part of her journey? (See page 108.) The Shepherd tells her that the delay is "not unto death, but for the glory of God" (p. 112). What does this mean, and how might this be an allegory of our own lives?

7. At the foot of the precipice of Mt. Injury, Much-Afraid, who is now more afraid than ever, is approached by Craven Fear. He plays on her fears by telling her to imagine, or picture, what it was going to be like on the trek up that very steep mountain (p.123). In Chapter Eleven (p. 145) the Shepherd tells her to not ever allow herself to do that. He says He will lead her through much danger and tribulation: "Even if I lead you through the Valley of the Shadow itself you need not fear . . . " (p. 144). How is it that sometimes we, in our fear, try to imagine what it will be like, and what is the danger in this?

8. In Chapter Ten Much-Afraid learns the second lesson of love: Bearing-the-Cost, or Forgiveness (p. 137). What was the significance of this little flower's situation? Is this an easy lesson to learn? Why? How does this lesson help her when she is in the storms and the mist? Which was worse for her, and why?

9. Chapter Twelve ends with the Shepherd asking Much-Afraid if she would be willing to trust him, even if everything in the world seemed to say that he had deceived her (p. 168). She replies, "My Lord, if you can deceive me, you may. It can make no difference" (p. 169). In Chapter Thirteen, her faith is ultimately tried in the Valley of Loss, where everything that had been gained up to that point would be lost, and she would have to begin again. It was the turning point in her decision to follow the Shepherd, or not. What was the significance of walking down the path of forgiveness into the Valley of Loss? See especially pages 172, 176, and 179.

10. In Chapter Fifteen, why must the natural longing for human love be replaced (p. 198, 199)? Discuss this in terms of the Biblical passage which states, "I loved Him because He first loved me." See pages 24–27; 226–227. How is it that our great need for love can bring us to Christ (p. 249), and then His love transform us? See Chapters Nineteen and Twenty.

Discussion Guide

The Screwtape Letters by C. S. Lewis

ISBN 0-060-65293-4 ❧ Zondervan/HarperCollins
160 pages ❧ theological fantasy

1. Discuss symbols of evil, or the devil in our culture. How do these effect how we think about evil and/or the devil? How do these popular notions differ from what Lewis has depicted in his devil, Screwtape?

2. Discuss the significance of C. S. Lewis using the name "Wormwood" for his fiendish devil (Wood worms feed on living wood, destroying it from the inside.)

3. The plot of *Screwtape* is not to tell a story, but to show the psychology of temptation from the point of hell. The young man under temptation could be *Anyone*, and the plot is the ultimate salvation or damnation of every individual. By using this formula, how does Lewis make us understand the human condition? If Screwtape were writing a letter about you, what personality flaw might he zero in on, and what psychology might he use to keep you "out of the Enemy's clutches?"

4. Which Screwtape letter most poignantly spoke to you, or bothered you, and why?

5. In Screwtape's view, are there any particular crucial sins which ought to be developed in a person, and why? What sorts of attitudes is Screwtape most interested in getting Wormwood to foster in the man he is tempting?

6. Discuss some of the back-handed compliments that Screwtape pays to God, and his statements about trying to find out what "the Enemy" is really up to! What qualities of "the Enemy" does Screwtape confess stump him?

7. What reports back from Wormwood worry Screwtape and why? What reports didn't worry Screwtape and why? Did any of Screwtape's responses surprise you? Explain.

8. "A being which can still love is not yet a devil." Lewis, writing from this precept, and not the precept that devils are engaged in a pursuit of something called Evil, says that bad angels are motivated by

two things: First is their fear of punishment, and second is a kind of hunger. On Earth we have seen a desire or passion to dominate, to make another's intellectual and emotional life an extension of one's own. This desire is often called "Love." For devils the hunger is more ravenous. Satan desires to devour human souls, as opposed to God's Love which is to turn servants into sons intact with their full individuality (see Preface, pp. 8–9, & 41). Discuss how this corrupt passion is played out in Screwtape's letters to Wormwood.

9. Using an incident from one of these letters, explain how evil, or something that is bad, can be used to produce good. Could there be such a thing as "necessary" evil?

10. Name one thing in your life that you unreasonably fear, and then try to exaggerate the situation to the point of absurdity! In other words, have you ever been able to confront one of your demons and turn it into a joke?

11. What effect overall, if any, did reading this book have on you? How might this book have been different if Screwtape would have only been looking at, in individuals about to become Christians, what we normally think of as being the really big sins (for example: adultry, fornication, homosexuality, the practice of withcraft, etc.)?

Discussion Guide

In His Steps by Charles Sheldon

ISBN 1-59310-682-3 ᙍ Barbour Publishing
254 pages ᙍ historical fiction/revival sermon series

1. What is your emotional response to this book? Did it challenge you? Read and discuss I Peter 2:21 and Luke 15:27.

2. If you choose to follow *In His Steps*, where do you envision yourself in five years? Would it change your life?

3. Some people might be guilty of reducing all of the teachings of the Bible into what Jesus would do, or rather just the Gospels. What else of importance about Christianity does the Bible teach besides this idea? Consider both the Old and New Testaments. Also, are there things that we can do that Jesus would not have done?

4. Do you feel that WWJD has become so cliché due to mass marketing that it has lost its meaning, or do you think it is still powerful, especially to young people?

5. Was it a good idea to suggest that this commitment be for a year?

6. Edward Norman, the newspaper editor, faced his work with feelings of fear. Is it feasible to run a newspaper on such ideals as WWJD? What would be your feelings in a similar situation?

7. Discuss which problem you would find harder to resolve, how Rachael should use her talent, or how Virginia should use her wealth? How much does money have to do with answering the WWJD question? (See Mark 10:21) Would someone who is very poor be able to get anything out of this story? Explain.

8. Would your family influence you positively or negatively if you chose to follow in Jesus' steps? Might your family and friends view you as a religious fanatic? Explain.

9. Maxwell and Milton Wright both listed concrete things Jesus would probably do in their position. What are 5 things Christ might do in your position?

10. Rachael said with conviction that "I want to do something that will cost me something in the way of sacrifice." Have you experienced similar feelings regarding your relationship to Christ?

11. Is it easier to be called by God to work among the poor or to be challenged to minister to the more privileged class like Rollin Page was? Explain.

12. "Never before had Rev. Calvin Bruce realized how deep the feelings of his members flowed. He humbly confessed that the appeal he had made met with an unexpected response from men and women who . . . were hungry for something in their lives that the conventional type of church membership and fellowship had failed to give them." What do you think ministers would find is true about church members today?

13. If Christians feel called to minister to deprived areas of our major cities, how important is it that they actually live in these neighborhoods?

14. How relevant was Maxwell's sermon when he preached to the crowd in Chicago about the call for a new discipleship? (See pages 235–238 for a discussion): "There is a great quantity of nominal Christianity today. There is a need of more of the real kind. We need revival of the Christianity of Christ. We have unconsciously, lazily, selfishly, formally grown into a discipleship that Jesus himself would not acknowledge . . . [I]f our definition of being a Christian is simply to enjoy the privileges of worship, [to] be generous at no expense to ourselves, [to] have a good, easy time surrounded by pleasant friends and by comfortable things, [to] live respectably and at the same time avoid the world's great stress of sin and trouble because it is too much to bear it, . . . surely we are a long way from following the steps of [Jesus] . . ."

Discussion Guide

A Requiem For Love by Calvin Miller

ISBN 0-8499-0687-3 ❧ Word Publishing
152 pages ❧ "epic" poem/allegory of Genesis 2–3

1. From Chapter I, discuss how Satan might have felt waiting outside the garden on the day that God breathed life into man. Discuss Miller's portrayal of Satan on that day, and his conversation with God. What do you learn about Satan's character? How is it the same as or different from Lewis' Screwtape?

2. From Chapter II (& following), discuss the importance of man worshipping God, according to Miller. In what ways do we, and can we, worship God today?

3. From Chapter III (p. 20 & 26), discuss the difference between the philosophy "I *touch*, therefore I am" (*Tango ergo sum*), versus the philosophy of Descartes, "I *think*, therefore I am" (*Cognito ergo sum*). Which one do you believe is more important to man's spiritual well-being? Explain.

4. From Chapters IV & V, what was the purpose of God's gift of "love's full ecstasy" to Regis and Regina? What did Satan predict man would do with this gift? Today we live in a culture that believes lust and love are one and the same thing. How does this perversion affect our understanding of God's love and our desire to worship Him?

5. From Chapter VI, explain what Miller means when he says, "All being bears a weight/Proportioned to its size." What was God's burden when He created man to choose, and what is man's burden when he makes choices?

6. From Chapter VII, discuss the difference between the "power of love" as taught by God, versus "the love of power" as encouraged by Satan. How is love like power's opposite, humility, and how is knowledge, power?

7. From Chapter VIII, explain what Miller means when he says, "Love smiles./Hate grins." Also, what is it that Satan tells Regina about clothes? Discuss the truth in what he says (p.60). Has there

ever been a time when this was not true except for in the Garden of Eden?

8. From Chapter IX & X, Satan poisons Regina's imagination with a lust for power, for beauty, for wealth, and for him! He promises that he will give her all of these things if she will call love, hate. Miller calls this the greatest sin. Explain. How is it that we do this? Recall Chapter XVIII (p. 114) when she begins to question God's decisions. According to Miller, what should man do to avoid this?

9. From Chapters XII & XIII, God placed a spade and a hoe under the morning tree, while Satan placed a crown and a mirror under the sunset tree. Discuss the sin of vanity and its results. How does your own vanity cause you to sin? Discuss in what ways work might be the opposite of vanity. Discuss how it became easier for Satan to appeal to Regina once she had more self-awareness, or vanity.

10. From Chapter XIV, discuss how it is that hate comes easier than love, or is this one of Satan's lies?

11. From Chapter XV, both Regis and Regina ask God to remove Satan from the garden, but God tells them that he is there only by their request: "He came here at your will./He will go of his accord/When you desire him gone" (p. 100). They denied this saying that they had never asked him in this place. God reminds them that what they harbor in their hearts their tongues would scorn to speak aloud." How often in our hearts do we call on Satan to enter our lives, even though we would deny that we do? What might be an example of this?

12. From Chapters XVI–XIX, discuss the effect that spending time with Satan has on Regina. The Biblical account never relates how long it took Satan to convince Eve to eat of the fruit from the tree of the knowledge of good and evil. How long do you think it might have taken someone who walked and talked with God so regularly? How long do you think it might have taken you? Why?

13. From Chapter XX, discuss Satan's explanation as to why Regis would eat the forbidden fruit after he finds out that Regina has eaten it: "He will not permit in you/What he does not find within himself." Is there any truth to this in terms of how we choose mates for ourselves? Why do you think Satan might have spent so much time with Regina (Eve), and less with Regis (Adam)? What was her weakness that made her find Satan so appealing?

14. From Chapters XIX and XX, Satan tells Regina that in disobedi-
    ence there is often ecstasy and exhilaration, and after eating the
    forbidden fruit she felt this ecstasy, though for only a moment,
    until she suddenly felt both alone and naked, which she knew to
    be God's judgment. Discuss why it is that committing a sin can be
    so exhilarating, and what it means to be "alone" and "naked."

15. Chapter XXI is Regina's lament, or her requiem for love. A
    "Requiem" is a song for the dead. Why is this such a fitting title for
    this work?

16. From Chapter XXII, one thing this work does is make it more
    understandable as to why Adam ate the forbidden fruit. Discuss
    Miller's interpretation of the choice that lay before Regis. Why did
    he choose his wife instead of his Father? What choice do you think
    you would have made? What choice do you think your spouse
    would make? Have you ever been tempted to "fall short" when a
    loved one has? Discuss a situation when this might be a particularly
    difficult temptation.

17. In Chapter XXIII the World-Hater mocks the Earthmaker for
    what His creation has done by being allowed to choose. He says
    that "Now they hate so far only me/But soon perhaps each other/
    And, oh, the glorious hate of all their descendants." While their
    fallenness delights Satan, God still feels love, and thus gives them
    both reassurance. Do you see the story (of Adam and Eve) as a
    happy one or as a tragedy? Explain.

18. Do you like what Calvin Miller has done to the story of Adam
    and Eve from Genesis, or not? What would you change about it
    if you were writing it? What would you particularly want to keep?
    Explain both answers.

Discussion Guide

At Home in Mitford by Jan Karon

ISBN 0-14-025448-X ∽ Penguin Books
446 pages ∽ *NY Times* Bestseller fiction

1. What character did you like the most, and why? What character, if any, did you dislike at first, but later come to appreciate or understand?

2. What role does Barnabas play in Father Tim's life? What other characters invade Father Tim's life, but eventually prove to be enriching? Is there anyone who brings him down? How does Father Tim come to terms with that?

3. How does Dooley contribute to Father Tim's life? Do you have someone like Dooley in your own life?

4. Miss Sadie and Miss Rose are very different characters, but both make a powerful and unique contribution to the story. What makes them such vivid characters?

5. Priests and ministers seldom have people they can talk to in confidence. Who becomes this person for Father Tim? What kinds of personal stuff does he confide? What role does prayer play in giving Father Tim a chance to vent his true feelings?

6. Discuss the nature of faith and obedience to God in Father Tim's life. What role does prayer play in Father Tim's faith?

7. Do Jan Karon's characters remind you of any people you know such as your neighbors or relatives?

8. What function does a place like the Main Street Grill fill in a town? Where do you get your town news? Where are you most often likely to run into your friends and neighbors?

9. Do you think you could find Mitford anywhere, or do you feel that the setting and people are too storybook, and unrealistic?

Discussion Guide

A Skeleton in God's Closet by Paul Maier

ISBN 0-8407-3424-7 ∽ Thomas Nelson Publishers
336 pages ∽ mystery/thriller

". . . and if Christ is not raised, your faith has been in vain."
I Corinthians 15:12–19

1. Should anybody ever be afraid of the truth, no matter what it is? Should we be willing to investigate things that may challenge our faith? (Several times in the story different people express a desire to destroy the evidence that they believe will prove Jesus did not literally rise from the dead. Also, several times it is stated that all that matters is what people think is true.) Ultimately truth cannot be destroyed, but our concept of it can be. Would you have wanted the evidence destroyed if it meant a possibility of it being the bones of Jesus? (page 133, 169, 223)

2. What is faith? Is faith "blind," or can it be based on knowledge and evidence? Or, can it be based on both knowledge and trust? Discuss.

3. What did you learn about archaeology as a science that can prove or disprove parts of the Bible?

4. Would a discovery such as this have the effect on Christianity that is suggested in this story? Look at other scenarios: Would finding Noah's Ark prove to the world anything? Did Christ's miracles change everyone's faith? What about the story of the rich man and Lazarus? (Luke 16:19–31). Even seeing Jesus risen from the dead and seeing the empty tomb did not convince everyone!

5. There is much evidence to prove Christ's resurrection (also see page 253–54), but why is it so important that Jesus be raised from the dead?

6. What are some of the economic and political effects that Christianity has had on the world?

7. What was Jennings' motivation to plant this hoax? (It goes back to the basic problem of evil. "Evil disproves God." See pages 162 and 313.) How do we explain the problem of evil?

8. Do you think this story would play itself out in real life the way it's written? For example, would people really try to commit suicide, or murder? Would as many people be as upset as the author suggests? Would people believe that the end was upon us? Would they believe the archaeologists to be Anti-Christs? Would church attendance drastically decline? Would there be people trying to profit from such a crisis as this? (pp. 130, 155–157, 165–167)

9. How might the effect on everyone's faith of discovering Jesus' bones compare to the effect of Darwin's work, *The Origin of the Species*, published in 1859, "proving" evolution, on people in the nineteenth century? What might some other challenges be to a person's faith? Has your own faith ever been challenged? Explain.

10. Some people are very hostile towards any form of apologetics (the defense of Christianity). There is a bumper sticker that says: "God said it, I believe it, that settles it." What's wrong with this "philosophy"? How would this apply to *A Skeleton in God's Closet*?

11. This novel also revolves around the importance to Christianity of a physical resurrection of Jesus. How else would you explain the empty tomb? That would have had to have been a hoax, therefore making a lie out of what Jesus said he would do, and thus weakening all of Christianity. Read the following scriptures as references for this story: Matthew 16:21, 17:23, 20:17, 27:62–64 and Luke 9:22, 24:7–12, 24:21–23. Would it make a difference to your faith and to Christianity if Christ had not physically resurrected?

Discussion Guide

The Scarlet Letter by Nathaniel Hawthorne

ISBN 0-553-21009-2 ✌ Bantam Classic

240 pages ✌ American literary classic "romance"

1. Discuss the three main ideas, or themes, explored in this romance: adultery, hypocrisy, and revenge.

2. How is Hawthorne's concept of romance like that of other writers? Of course he includes adventurous action, heroic characters, picturesque settings. He even includes mysterious events, as well as scenes and ideas that are generally considered remote from everyday, common life. Discuss these elements, as well as how some of his concepts about a romance novel might differ?

3. We know that one of Nathaniel Hawthorne's ancestor's, John Hathorne (the original spelling of his name; Nathaniel changed the spelling during his youth), was one of the three judges at the Salem witch trials of 1692. Consider Hawthorne's view toward Puritanism. Did he approve or disapprove of it? Do you feel that he is criticizing the Puritans' bigotry? Explain. Since Hester is the heroine, what is it that Hawthorne approves of in her character?

4. James 5:16 says to "Confess your faults to one another, and pray for one another, that ye may be healed," and the Puritans took this quite seriously. Dimmesdale is too weak to do what he knows is required of him, and so during his seven years of silence he adds the sin of hypocrisy. Today we would say that he rationalized (p. 121–122). How did his silence hurt and help him, and how did Hester's confession hurt and help her? Do you believe that Dimmesdale's confession came too late? Explain.

5. What are your feelings about public confessions in general? Discuss some of the extremes that we as a culture have taken the idea of public "confession." (examples: Bill Clinton's public confession about having sex, "confessional" TV talk shows)

6. Do you feel that Hawthorne has "romanticized" Hester's adultery? Hester could have chosen to return to England to live, but she chooses to stay in Boston. Why? Do you agree or disagree with her decision?

7. Discuss Hester's purification through repentance in this novel. Discuss how she changes as a woman, both outwardly and inwardly. Discuss the function of the symbolism of wearing the letter "A".

8. It may be said that Roger Chillingsworth commits the greatest sin. What is that, and do you agree? (see esp. p. 117–118) Explain.

9. The community is responsible for the action in Chapters I–VIII, Chillingsworth then becomes responsible for the action in IX–XII, Hester in XIII–XX, and Dimmesdale in XXI–XXIV. Discuss how this becomes so, and why.

10. Discuss how the chief points of Puritan theology are played out in this novel: (1) Absolute sovereignty of God. (2) Predestination. An omniscient Deity knows from the beginning who will be saved. (3) Providence. God directly intervenes in the world. (4) Natural depravity. Since Adam's fall all men are born in sin and deserve damnation. (5) Election. Through God's mercy a few are saved, but by grace alone, not by their efforts. (6) Evil is inner. Man needs reform of himself. (7) God is revealed in the Bible.

Discussion Guide

The Christmas Cross by Max Lucado

ISBN 0-8499-1546-5 ❧ Word Publishing

49 pages ❧ holiday fiction

1. This is a story about irrevocable mistakes made in life, even twice in one lifetime. Do you think it is plausible that after hearing Joe's story the narrator could have understood and been so forgiving? Could you have?

2. How did hearing Joe's story enable the narrator to get over his anger at his wife, Meg?

3. Carving the nativity scene and the face of the baby Messiah had an effect on Ottolman so that he wanted to go to church and find out about Jesus. Explain the message of the first sermon he heard as a believer—"Born Crucified," and how it might have contained in it a message that would ease the pain he carried around inside himself.

4. What was the sin that Carmen committed that Ottolman could not forgive? Whose forgiveness in the end was greater, Ottolman's or Carmen's? Why is it so important that we be able to forgive each other?

5. Do you think it was all right that when Ottolman returned the baby Jesus to the nativity scene that he never returned the scarlet cross? What did that cross represent to him?

6. Do you feel that the interactive features and beautiful artwork in this book helped make the story more powerful? Explain.

Sample Syllabus II

1. *Tuesdays With Morrie* by Mitch Albom

A true story that chronicles one man's love for his teacher and mentor. Morrie Schwartz, Mitch's college professor nearly twenty years ago, is dying. Seeing Morrie's illness covered on "Nightline," Mitch rekindles their relationship, meeting with Morrie every Tuesday, just as they used to in college, turning their relationship into one final "class" lesson on how to live.

2. *Redeeming Love* by Francine Rivers

A powerful retelling of the Old Testament Book of Hosea, set in 1850s California. Angel, who was sold into prostitution as a child, survives by keeping alive her hatred of the men who use her. Then she meets Michael Hosea, a man who seeks his Father's heart in everything, and thus obeying God's call to marry Angel and to love her unconditionally. Finally, despite her bitter resistance, her frozen heart begins to thaw, though not without overwhelming feelings of unworthiness and fear. Her final healing must come from the One who loves her even more than Michael Hosea does.

3. *The Great Divorce* by C. S. Lewis

This classic work of fantasy offers a vision of the Afterworld, as the narrator boards a bus on a dreary afternoon and embarks on an incredible journey through Heaven and Hell. He meets a host of supernatural beings far removed from his expectations, and comes to some significant realizations about the nature of good and evil.

4. *The Believers* by Janice Holt

This historical novel set in 1800s Kentucky, is a story about love and marriage set in a Shaker community. Rebecca Fowler is only seventeen when she marries her first love, Richard Cooper. It is only after their first child is stillborn that Richard begins to show signs of religious fanaticism in his insistence that it is God's punishment visited upon them, thus the Shaker missionaries newly arrived in Kentucky from New York find him an easy convert. Though they join the Shaker community together, once there they must live apart. As time passes and Richard becomes strictly a "brother" to Rachel, and being unable to accept the doctrine of the Shakers, she finally finds the courage to follow the dictates of her heart.

5. *The Blue Bottle Club* by Penelope J. Stokes

This is a story of four strong women who follow their dreams even when life throws a wrench into their plans. They learn that God can bring beauty out of sorrow and pain. In the dim stillness of the Cameron's dusty attic, four teenage friends, with their dreams written down on paper and stashed inside a blue cobalt bottle, join hands and commit their dreams to the future: Letitia dreams of marriage to her high school sweetheart, Mary Love hopes to become a famous artist, wealthy Eleanor aspires to help those in need as a social worker, and Adora, the preacher's daughter, yearns to be a Hollywood film star.

6. *The Poisonwood Bible* by Barbara Kingsolver

This story is told by the wife and four daughters of a fiery evangelical Baptist missionary, Nathan Price, who find themselves in the Belgian Congo in 1959. Everything they have carried with them becomes useless on African soil, and we watch the epic of one family's tragic undoing over the course of three decades, played out against the bloody backdrop of Congo's political struggles, and woven in between threads of religion, race, sin, and redemption.

7. *Spoon River Anthology* by Edgar Lee Masters

An American classic book of dramatic monologues written in free verse, set in a 1915 Midwestern town where shocking scandals and secret tragedies are revealed by the dead citizens of the village cemetery who offer testimony about their lives. Corrupt as any big city, Spoon River is home to murderers, drunkards, crooked bankers, lechers, bitter wives, failed dreamers, plus a few good souls.

8. *Joshua* by Joseph Girzone

This truly spiritual story is a modern parable of Jesus set in today's time. Joshua moves to a small cabin on the edge of town, and the local people are at first mystified, then confused and disturbed by his presence. He is a quiet, simple man who supports himself solely by carpentry and woodworking.

9. *A Choice to Cherish* by Alan Maki

Alan spends a cold Montana Christmas with his dying grandfather, George, who opens a safe containing eight keepsakes. He tells Alan that he may select one as a gift, but before making his choice he must read a story each day that his grandfather has written previously about each item. Through these stories, Alan learns the secrets of his grandfather's life, and the reasons behind a family breach.

Discussion Guide

Tuesdays with Morrie by Mitch Albom

ISBN 0-385-48451-8 ⌘ Doubleday
192 pages ⌘ memoir

*". . . I have learned the secret of being content
in any and every situation . . ."*
Phil. 4:12

*"You have turned my wailing into dancing;
you removed my sackcloth and clothed me with joy."*
Ps. 30:11

1. This rather short little book about aging and dying has captured the hearts of millions of Americans. Why do you think that is?

2. In what ways did this final "class" with Morrie Schwartz change Mitch Albom? In what ways was Mitch different from Morrie?

3. What was the biggest lesson that you took away from reading this book?

4. Discuss the significance of the story Mitch recalls from his childhood of sledding and almost getting hit by a car (pp. 98–99). Why would he include that story in a book like this?

5. Discuss what Morrie means about detaching himself from experience (pp. 103–106) in order to find peacefulness and serenity. Have you ever been able to do this? Do you think it would be something beneficial to learn?

6. Morrie talks about our culture's fear of aging, and Mitch recalls having counted the billboards of beautiful and youthful people on his way to the Boston airport. On the flip side, Morrie says that aging is not just decay, but that it is growth. (pp. 117–121) Discuss this. Have you ever been afraid of aging, and if so, what were you afraid of? Has your concept of aging changed over the years? Explain.

7. How would you feel about having a "living funeral"? How would you feel about attending one? (pp. 12–13)

8. This book is so much about how to live, but it is also about how to die. Both life and death have a way of inducing humility (pp. 21–22), and many of the descriptions in this book bring us "face to face" with Morrie's physical decline. What part of this book did you find painful, or even shameful to read and why? How has life humbled you in ways you may not have expected?

9. Mitch asked Morrie, towards the end, if he had one perfectly healthy 24-hour day how he would want to spend it (p. 175). Mitch was at first surprised by Morrie's simplistic response, until he realized that it was the perfect response in light of Morrie's perspective on living. Do you think that it is possible to dream of the "perfect" day when you are young and healthy differently than you might think of it when you are dying? How has your idea of the perfect day changed from when you were younger?

10. Finally, is there anything in your life that you plan to change after having read this book, like for example, dance more, or just plain be more joyful? (By the way, is there any outward visible sign of joy by which people would remember you?) Ecc. 8:15 "So I commend the enjoyment of life, because nothing is better for a man under the sun than to eat and drink and be glad. Then joy will accompany him in his work all the days of the life God has given him under the sun."

Discussion Guide

Redeeming Love by Francine Rivers

ISBN 1-57673-186-3 ∾ Alabaster/Multnomah Women's Fiction
464 pages ∾ historical romance

1. Discuss what makes this romance novel different from say, a Harlequin Romance, a Jackie Collins or Barbara Cartland novel, or something like it? Why do you think women, who have always been the number one marketing target for these books, are so interested in reading them? Do you think they present a warped concept of love? Discuss.

2. One of the most frustrating elements in this story is Angel's refusal to accept Michael's love. Why do you think it is so hard for her to give in? Also, how could her refusal to accept Michael's love be like a person's refusal to accept Christ's love?

3. In what way(s) is Michael too good to be true? Do you feel his "perfect" love hurt or helped the story? How is Michael's love for Angel like God's love for us? Remember Romans 5:8 that reads, "But God demonstrates His own love for us in this: While we were still sinners, Christ died for us."

4. Discuss the character of Michael's brother-in-law, Paul. Why does he feel the way he does, and how might we sometimes be like him?

5. Discuss the role of the Altman family in Angel's life. Why is Angel so afraid of them at first? Is she afraid that they might use I Corinthians 6:9–11 against her?

6. Discuss the character of the Doctor who intervenes in Angel's life. Would you have done what he did? Better yet, if a known prostitute would join your church, confess, and get baptized, would you go down to her, shake her hand, and welcome her as a sister? Why or why not?

7. Discuss the character of the pimp, Duke. What kind of hold did he have on Angel? What might he represent in your life?

8. Do you feel that River's portrayal of such a painful issue was necessary or unnecessary to the message of the story? Explain.

9. Discuss how the meaning of God's Grace is played out in this novel.

10. How does the Christian message in this story differ from the message in *The Scarlet Letter*?

11. When Angel is finally able to reject her life of sin, she does not reject the other women who are still involved in the life of prostitution. How might God be able to use your new life to reach out to people from your old life? Do we oftentimes have too much fear that a person might slip back into their old ways? What made this last time "it" for Angel?

12. Discuss the meaningfulness of the scene when Angel returns to Michael the final time? How is that symbolic of how we will stand before Christ?

13. What is the strongest spiritual insight that you took away with you after reading this book?

Discussion Guide

The Great Divorce by C. S. Lewis

ISBN 0-060-65295-0 ❧ Zondervan/HarperCollins
160 pages ❧ religious fantasy

1. This work is partly an examination of the nature of good and evil, and the insistence that finally the two may not exist together, that it must be "either-or" (see the Preface). What particularly is the nature of evil as it is portrayed by Lewis?

2. Discuss the issue of "free-will" (see page 72) as being a major theme of this work.

3. Discuss some of the sins that are keeping the souls out of Heaven (for example: false pride, possessive love, lustfulness, cynicism & doubt, self-pity, grumbling, materialism, etc.).

4. The man who committed murder said that murder was not his worst sin, but that hatred was. Discuss this (pages 33–36). Could we be mistaken when we put into a hierarchy the sins we believe to be the greatest, or the least likely to be forgiven or recovered from? How might we be fooling ourselves?

5. Our existence on this earth is what we have philosophically been taught to believe to be Reality. Discuss Lewis' idea that compared to heaven we are merely shadows, or ghosts. This is also the concept that Plato expressed in his *Republic* with the story of the cave. Do you find this idea appealing and hopeful, or do you find it appalling and negative?

6. How did the work challenge your imagination as to what heaven or hell might be like? Compare Lewis' depictions to those in the Book of Revelations.

7. Discuss the idea that heaven and hell will both reach all the way back into eternity (page 11).

8. Lewis discusses the idea with MacDonald of the action of pity versus the passion of pity. Discuss the difference. (pages 117–120) Why does the passion of pity belong in Hell?

9. Discuss the paragraph on page 96 when MacDonald is explaining to Lewis that the false religion of lust is baser than the false religion of mother-love or patriotism or art, but that lust is less likely to be

made into a religion. What did he mean? Do you agree? (See question #6.)

10. What effect does it have on the story to find out in the end that the whole thing was a dream?

Discussion Guide

The Believers by Janice Holt Giles

ISBN 0-8131-0189-1 ☙ UK Press
214 pages ☙ historical fiction

1. What did you learn about the Shakers that you didn't already know? Do you think that current culture has over-romanticized Shaker life? Do you think that Giles was too biased against the Shakers, especially since the reader's sympathy is with the character who leaves?

2. What interest do you think Mother Ann Lee had in starting such a religious "utopian" community that had such strict rules about celibacy?

3. What were some of the appeals of Shaker life that drew members into the Shaker community?

4. Discuss the different ways in which Shaker life affected the many female characters. Some were happy in the community. Why?

5. The State of Kentucky passed legislation that granted immediate divorce to any parties who were disenchanted with their spouses' Shaker convictions (vii). Do you think that it was okay for Rebecca to divorce Richard and marry Stephen? Do you think she should have done it much sooner, and if so, why do you think she didn't?

6. What were some of the problems with the organization of "artificial families"?

7. Do you think that Richard's inner character and make-up, as well as the outer circumstances, affected the way he reacted in terms of his convictions to Shaker life? Not everyone seemed as strongly convicted as Richard? Why not?

8. Do you think that Rebecca or Richard's parents could have done anything to prevent what their children did? In the Preface, Cecilia Macheski mentions the general belief during this time in the idea of Manifest Destiny (xi), and thus the acceptance of westward movement and expansion, which meant that there was always the possibility that one's children might leave home and move far away, maybe never to see their families again.

9. Discuss the characterization and treatment of Jency as a negative stereotype of a black slave. Remember that the book was written in 1954. Does that make a difference?

Discussion Guide

The Blue Bottle Club by Penelope J. Stokes
ISBN 0-8499-3780-9 ∽ Word Publishing
345 pages ∽ fiction

1. With which character did you most identify: Letitia (wanted marriage to her high school sweetheart and children), Mary Love (wanted a life dedicated to her art), Eleanor (wanted a life as a social worker), or Adora (a preacher's daughter who dreamed of stardom in Hollywood)? Explain.

2. Sometimes before we can truly stand before God we must go through the purifying fire of suffering and self-denial. As painful as this may be, we learn that God is always with us, working to refine our faith and strengthen our trust in Him. Why is it that sometimes we have to be brought to our knees in order to look up and see the One who is truly in control of our lives? Discuss this in terms of the characters in the book, including Brendan Delaney, the reporter.

3. Our natural inclination is to go our own ways and follow our dreams. How might we start with a dream that God planted in us, and then have it see fruition in a way that we may not have expected? Do you think that every dream in its fulfillment should be about bringing others to God? Have you or anyone you have ever known followed a dream that turned out differently than expected, and yet reached a destiny unimagined? How did God mold you (or someone else) so that you were able to fulfill your dream/destiny? Have you ever had to give up a dream?

4. Do you think there were any flaws in the story such as that maybe the author tried too hard to tie up loose ends in Brendan's life? Brendan is only in her 30s, whereas the members of the Blue Bottle Club are in their 80s! How would you finish writing Brendan's story?

5. What role do you think the Depression era of the 1930's played in the development of these women's lives?

6. Do you think that a story like this could inspire you to want to live each day to the fullest, trusting each day in God? How so?

7. Discuss this book in terms of its being a celebration of women, of their strengths, their weaknesses, and their potential to be what God designed them to be.

Discussion Guide

Spoon River Anthology by Edgar Lee Masters

ISBN 0-451-52530-2 ∞ Signet Classic
284 pages / free verse ∞ American Classic

*"Do you show your wonders to the dead? Do those who are dead rise up
and praise you? Is your love declared in the grave, your faithfulness in
Destruction? Are your wonders known in the place of darkness, or your
righteous deeds in the land of oblivion?"*
Ps 88:10–12

1. The American myth of the moral superiority of small-town life
   is dispelled in this collection of dramatic monologues spoken by
   Spoon River's dead citizens. In 1915, when this work was published, what would have been the myth of the small town, and do
   you think it still exists today?

2. Per capita, there seem to be more churches in small towns than in
   larger cities. Do you think this plays into the myth of small town
   moral superiority? How do you think this effects the way we see
   the need for evangelism in rural areas?

3. By 1915 the movement known as Realism was dominating the literary scene, which was a reaction to the Romantics, who depicted
   life more as we wished it to be, more picturesque, more adventurous, and more heroic. The Realists tried to present a more accurate
   imitation of life as it is. However, sometimes Realists set out to
   present the illusion that their fiction reflected life and the social
   world as it seemed to the common reader. As you read *Spoon River
   Anthology* did you feel as though its author was accurately depicting lives of small town people? Which monologue most reminded
   you of someone that you know, or know of? Which one did you
   feel most represented your life? Whose did you feel was the most
   tragic? The most despicable?

4. There exist two conflicting theories about the nature of man. One
   insists that man is basically good, the other argues that man is basically evil. Which theory do you believe fiction most often reflects?
   Which type of fiction are you most drawn to, the kind that in the
   end makes you feel like everyone is basically good, or the kind that

says, no, man is evil? What is the danger of buying into the "man is good" theory? Or vice versa? Discuss this in terms of small town moral superiority. (Compare Spoon River to Mitford.)

5. *Spoon River Anthology* is written in such a dramatic form that readers might feel like they are being let in on secrets, because the lives of the townspeople only unfold as each one tells on himself, or on someone else. The reader is able to gather information about individual people, about families, and about the economic, political, and social structure of the town. Several times someone's story undercuts someone else's. Many times there are confessions, or naive or devious expressions; there is irony, and there are pleas. How many different scandals and tragedies, or good deeds, can you recall being revealed in this work? (Also, discuss this in terms of the above scripture.) How many citizens from different walks of life can you recall being depicted? Finally, discuss what you learned about this town, and how did this type of storytelling differ from the single-narrated, plot driven form you are used to reading? Did you find this an enjoyable format?

6. Lots of people probably have a shameful secret they hope to take to the grave, yet, many human tragedies are taken to the grave as well. Discuss what you think God sees when He looks down on our town, or on the world, as opposed to what we "saw" when we read about the people of Spoon River? What would our town's anthology read like? And, most importantly, what would your epitaph reveal about you?

Discussion Guide

Joshua by Joseph F. Girzone

ISBN 0-02-019890-6 ᐯᕋ Collier Books/MacMillan Publishing
271 pages ᐯᕋ parable
Concerning what Jesus said about speaking in parables,
Read Matthew 13:34–35; Mark 4:10–12, 33–34

1. In what ways, if any, did this story help you to get a better under-standing of the person of Jesus? How could you use *Joshua* as an evangelistic tool to talk to someone about Jesus?

2. If a parable is a teaching device, what is the lesson in this story? Why is it so inspirational?

3. Discuss the similarities between the story of Joshua and the gospels' account of the life of Jesus (for example, Marcia and Mary Magdalen).

4. Discuss the significance of the woodcarvings of the apostle Peter for the Anglican priest, Father Jeremy Darby, and the pastor of a black congregation, Rev. Osgood Rowland. What was the message of each statue? Also, discuss how Christ knows us better than we know ourselves and is able to give us what we need, even when we don't initially see it. Has this ever happened to you?

5. Discuss reasons why Jesus spoke both to the masses and to in-dividuals in parables. (Story is not soft theology, but can express deep theological truths.) Also, discuss how Christ can use different artistic mediums to speak straight to the heart of individuals and move them closer to where he wants them to be.

6. Many of the Jews of Old were too wrapped up in their legalisms to accept Jesus the first time he came. Could there be a possibility that Christians have in many ways become like those ancient scribes and Pharisees (p.187, 194)?

7. Joshua speaks a lot about freedom for God's children (p. 215). How would you explain this to someone who sees the Church as a watchdog and policeman? See Galatians 5:1 "It is for freedom that Christ has set us free. Stand firm, then, and do not let yourselves be burdened again by a yoke of slavery." Verses 13–15: "You, my brothers, were called to be free. But do not use your freedom to indulge the sinful nature; rather, serve one another in love. The

entire law is summed up in one command: 'Love your neighbor as yourself.' If you keep on biting and devouring each other, watch out or you will be destroyed by each other."

8. Discuss what Joshua says about Christian denominations and how it is not their following of Jesus that makes them different from one another, but their denominational practices that make them different and keep them apart, thus bringing ridicule onto Christianity and destroying the united influence it could have on the world (p.102–103, 137). "Jesus prayed fervently that his people would be one. . ." (p. 137); see John 17:20–23 ". . . May they be brought to complete unity to let the world know that you sent me, and have loved them even as you have loved me." Non-believers don't care about our arguments, only the issue of Christ.

9. When Joshua is asked what he thinks about religion, he responds by asking, "What do you mean by religion? The way that it is, or the way that God intended it to be? There's a big difference, you know" (p. 73–75). Do you agree, and if so, in what way?

Discussion Guide

A Choice to Cherish by Alan Maki

ISBN 0-8054-2338-9 ∽ Broadman & Holman Publishers
184 pages ∽ holiday fiction

1. Grandpa George has eight "gifts" inside his safe that Alan is to choose one from on Christmas to be his: a baseball, a rifle, ten thousand dollars, a silver key to a 1972 Yamaha, an elk-ivory necklace, a marathon certificate, a Santa costume, and a bronze baby shoe. With each gift there is a story, and Alan is to read only two a day, before he makes his choice. Which story do you think moved Alan the most, and why? Which story moved you the most, and why?

2. What do the eight stories reveal about the tragedies and triumphs of George Maki's life, and what kind of man he was?

3. What is the message in this story concerning misunderstandings, grudges, and forgiveness?

4. Alan does not consider himself to be a Christian, though by the end of the story he accepts Jesus as well as his gift from Grandpa. Really, Alan received two gifts from Grandpa George. Discuss how it is that even in one's dying and in death God is able to use a person to bring someone to Christ. What was it about Grandpa's faith that Alan found so attractive?

5. As you read each one of the stories, what were your feelings concerning Alan's dad, Dale? What did you want to say to him? What about Alan's mother? Do you think she could have done more to ease the situation, or should she have just stayed out of it like she did?

6. At the beginning Alan did not really want to go to Montana and stay with his dying grandfather. After all, he was only 20 years old and had a life. How did this short visit change the character of Alan Maki?

7. What was Robin's role in this story? Have you ever found yourself in Robin's position, visiting with someone who had no close family? Would you be more apt to do so after having read this story?

Sample Syllabus III

1. *The Testament* by John Grisham

A story about a very rich, angry old man who is on his deathbed, decides to rewrite his will, leaving as his sole heir of his eleven billion dollar fortune, a mysterious woman named Rachel Lane. Nate O'Riley, a lawyer fresh out of rehab is sent into the jungles of Brazil to find her at any cost, while a vicious legal battle is about to begin, involving Troy's children, and ex-wives. What Nate discovers in Rachel will forever change his life.

2. *Till We Have Faces* by C. S. Lewis

This is the story of two princesses, one beautiful, and one ugly, and of the struggles between sacred and profane love. Reworking the classical myth of Psyche, a mortal woman with whom the god Cupid fell in love, and who was finally made immortal by Zeus, Lewis is not only able to paint a picture of the mystic union between the Church and Christ, but is able to illustrate what a jealous and self-centered love can do to one's heart without Christ.

3. *Bookends* by Liz Curtis Higgs

This is a light-hearted story about two people of Moravian background, Emilie and Jonas, who meet each other in a small Pennsylvania town. While she has come there to help her career by finding and preserving an original church structure—she has a Ph.D. in history—he is developing a golf course on that very spot of land. Of course the whole affair becomes a battle of wits between two people who are the exact opposites of each other, and before it is over will involve several other individuals, as well as an assortment of pets and plants!

4. *Ezekiel's Shadow* by David Ryan Long

After having spent time in Utah with a friend, best-selling author of horror novels, Ian Merchant, has a conversion experience that ends up in his suffering an identity crisis. Although everyone around him can see that he has changed, he questions himself as to whether he will ever be able to build a new life of faith when the sins of his past are lining the bookshelves of America. It seems that somebody is out to give him a lesson on what true horror is all about.

5. *Seaside* by Terri Blackstock

When two adult sisters, who both envy each other for the success and happiness they think the other one's got, are called by their mother to join her for a seaside vacation on the Gulf of Mexico, neither sister thinks she can take the time out of her busy schedule. Feeling a burdensome sense of duty, and a little guilt, the three of them spend what ends up being a very memorable week together. Little do the two sisters know what surprise and lessons await them.

6. *Winter Passing* by Cindy McCormick Martinusen

In 1941, a young woman hears her cell door open and realizes that her time has come to die at the hands of the Nazis. She will face execution so that her best friend since childhood, along with her friend's unborn child, might live. She will die in Celia's place, but she is not sorry. Sixty years later, Darby Evans must unravel the mysterious secrets, which envelop her dying grandmother's final wish. As Darby travels back to her grandmother's homeland of Austria, she comes to know the horrors of the Holocaust in a very personal way, and discovers a faith that transcends even the worst evil.

7. *Velma Still Cooks In Leeway* by Vinita Hampton Wright

Velma Brendle is the chief cook at Velma's diner in Leeway, Kansas, as well as the janitor at Jerusalem Baptist Church. However, like the townspeople whose burdens she carries on her shoulders, Velma also seeks to find purpose and healing in not only the events of her past, but in her everyday existence. This novel offers the hope that God is not only concerned about our lives, but that He uses whatever we are, and wherever we are to teach us so that we can grow in Him.

8. *The Immortal* by Angela Elwell Hunt

Asher has been wandering the earth for over 2,000 years, unable to die, suffering for and serving mankind, tortured by his belief that his sin against Jesus had been such that he could do no less than the one thing that would speed up Christ's return. This suspenseful, yet moving novel teaches us that we should not be so preoccupied with looking for Jesus to come back that we forget what his death and resurrection were about.

9. *One Shenandoah Winter* by T. Davis Bunn

In the late fall of 1961, Dr. Nathan Reynolds, a skilled specialist and an angry man, arrives at the small rural town of Hillsboro from Baltimore, Maryland. From the start he clashes with just about everyone, including the assistant Mayor, Connie Wilkes, who has troubles of her own. Not certain as to whether Nathan will stay in the town that so desperately needs him, Connie wishes she didn't care. However, before the first winter snowfall, a chain of events is set in motion that will transform Connie, the doctor, and the town forever, and by Christmas day, the greatest sorrow and the greatest miracle will bring about redemption to everyone.

Discussion Guide

The Testament by John Grisham

ISBN 0-440-23474-3 ✑ Island Books/Dell Publishing
533 pages ✑ *New York Times* Bestseller

"For the love of money is a root of all kinds of evil.
Some people, eager for money, have wandered from the faith and pierced
themselves with many griefs."
I Tim 6:10

"No one can serve two masters. Either he will hate the one and love the
other, or he will be devoted to the one and despise the other. You cannot
serve both God and Money."
Matt 6:24

"Whoever loves money never has money enough; whoever loves wealth
is never satisfied with his income. This too is meaningless."
Eccl 5:10

1. Discuss Troy Phelan and what he did to his children and ex-wives. Do you think Troy is a realistically portrayed character and antagonist? Did you feel any sympathy for him? Why or why not? To whom do you think he should have left his money?

2. Nate O'Riley feels some sympathy for the Phelan children, even though all the attorneys know that no jury ever would. How would you feel concerning them if you were a juror listening to this case?

3. Do you think Grisham was fair in his portrayal of Nate's conversion to Christianity? Do you believe that getting out of the courtroom was necessary?

4. How do you feel about the way Nate deposed the Phelan children, Snead, Nicolette, and the psychiatrists? As a Christian, should he have done anything differently? Why, or why not?

5. The message in this story seems to be that too much money corrupts totally. Do you agree or disagree, and what amount of money is "too much"? Do you think the inheritance would have corrupted Rachel Lane?

6. God promises never to tempt us with more than we can handle. Would inheriting $11 billion be too much of a temptation for you? Would winning $1 million in the lottery be too much?

7. The story's ending is somewhat surprising. How did you feel about Grisham emphasizing Nate's Christian "calling" instead of a promising future with Rachel Lane? Do you wish it would have ended differently with Rachel's character? If so, how would you have wanted it to end?

Discussion Guide

Till We Have Faces by C. S. Lewis

ISBN 0-15-690436-5 ∾ A Harvest Book/Harcourt Brace & Co.

309 pages ∾ mythic fiction

*"The heart is deceitful above all things and beyond cure. Who can under-
stand it? "I the Lord search the heart and examine the mind, to reward
a man according to his conduct, according to what his deeds deserve."*
Jeremiah 17:9–10

*"Nothing in all creation is hidden from God's sight.
Everything is uncovered and laid bare before the eyes of him
to whom we must give account."*
Hebrews 4:13

Psyche, in classical mythology, is the personification of the human soul.
She married Cupid, the god of love, and was made immortal by Zeus.
Here she is symbolic of Christ, as the perfect sacrifice, and as the Church
who is married to Christ in a mystic union. Venus (Roman) = Aphrodite
(Greek), goddess of love; Cupid (Roman) = Eros (Greek) god of love.
Ungit = a deformed or paganized version of Aphrodite, or Venus (in this
Christianized retelling of the myth); and The Shadowbrute = a deformed
or paganized version of Cupid (again, only in this Christianized retelling
of the myth)

   1. The Greeks had many words for love: *philia*, which had mostly to
      do with friendly affection, or love among equals; *eros*, which was
      erotic, passionate, boundless love as a husband and wife would
      share; *stergo*, which is the love of a parent or child, king or citizens,
      or any greater for lesser, or vice versa; and *agapa*, which in its noun
      form was only used after the birth of Christianity, and which re-
      fers to an unselfish, unconditional higher form of love. The Greeks
      most often referred to *eros* instead of *agapa* before Christianity
      when discussing godly love, thus partly an explanation for their
      pagan temple prostitutes. This is also a reason why Orual could not
      comprehend what Psyche was talking about in terms of her being
      married to a god. Discuss each of these types of love and how it is

exemplified in both its negative and positive extremes in *Till We Have Faces.*

2. Discuss the relationship between Orual and her father and how it plays into the overall theme of the story.

3. Discuss the conflict and final harmony between reason, represented by the Greek, Fox, and feeling and imagination, (and lack of reason) represented in Bardia. How does the belief in God require both reason and imagination? How could one without the other be harmful?

4. Discuss how Lewis incorporated Christian symbols and concepts into *Till We Have Faces.*

5. What does this story say about anyone standing before God on Judgment Day and having as an excuse that God left no sign of His existence? Orual had been given plenty of glimpses of god's existence, yet finally, when she could no longer deny that there was a god, her self-pity and pride and anger became her defenses against the truth. Compare this to some of the characters in Lewis' *The Great Divorce.*

6. Two elements of the love between God and man is sacrifice and obedience. Explain how Lewis incorporates these expressions into the Psyche myth.

7. Discuss the role of the high priest as seen in this story, versus Christ as High Priest (read Hebrews Chapter 5).

8. Explain what the god speaking to Orual meant when he said, "You also shall be Psyche" (p. 174 and p. 308).

9. Explain what Orual meant when she said that the gods do not speak to us openly; . . . "why should they hear the babble that we think we mean? How can they meet us face to face till we have faces?" (p. 294). Also, discuss the significance of Orual wearing a veil to cover her face throughout her adult life (see II Cor. 3:18).

10. What was Orual's complaint against the gods (p. 248–250), and what was their response to her? Was there any part of yourself that you saw in Orual? It is a humbling thought to realize that on the Day of Judgment we will be forced to see ourselves as God sees us. However, there is an encouraging final message in this story. What is it?

Discussion Guide

Bookends by Liz Curtis Higgs

ISBN 1-57673-611-3 ✑ Alabaster Books/Multnomah Publishers
334 pages ✑ contemporary fiction

1. After the story, in a letter to her readers, Higgs writes that the Moravians are fond of proclaiming as their watchword, "In essentials unity, in nonessentials liberty, and in all things love." She then states that this is a perfect rallying cry for the two main characters, Emilie Getz and Jonas Fielding. Explain what she means by that.

2. Emilie Getz remarks early in the story (p. 16) to Jonas that she was "born Moravian." He apparently has only been Moravian for five years, but we see in him a much deeper spirituality than we see in her. Like many people who are born into a church, she finally has to make the religion her own, that is, she must form a personal relationship with God. What, then, for Emilie becomes that climatic moment when God forces her to choose between following Him or her own desires (p. 239). What might have happened to her spiritually if she had chosen otherwise?

3. When Jonas is thinking about Emilie after he meets her, he thinks she is pretty and smart, though extremely cold natured. What the Lord tells him to do is to show her "fullness of joy," to show Emilie "who I am" (p. 43, 186–187). What is it about Jonas that God sees as obviously good for Emilie? What in their personalities make them exact opposites? What in their personalities compliment each other and are even the same? Discuss their relationship in terms of Psalms 16:11, "You have made known to me the path of life; you will fill me with joy in your presence; with external pleasures at your right hand." We need reminded every now and then that God wants us to experience joy! Which character, Emilie or Jonas, did you you most closely mirror?

4. There are several minor characters in the story who make quite an impact on the main characters' lives. One is Helen Bomberger (p. 27), the other is a younger woman named Beth Landis, who is the church secretary (p. 67). Discuss the importance of each woman's role in the story.

5. One of the biggest spiritual challenges in Jonas' life is his brother, Nate. Discuss your feelings about Nate and his rebelliousness against everything he'd been raised to believe, and then Jonas' decision to practice tough love on him in the end. How did this end up helping both brothers?

6. From the beginning of the story Jonas is trying to avoid a woman named Dee Dee. What is it about her that he dislikes, and do you think most single men would be "put off" by her? Did you expect Jonas to give in to her approaches ever? Why or why not? How did you feel about her in the beginning of the story, and did that ever change?

7. *Bookends* is a very charming and delightful story. What did you find to be some of the funniest moments between Emilie and Jonas? Were there any other incidents in the story which made you want to laugh? Explain.

8. Higgs set *Bookends* against the backdrop of a community of Moravians. What were some of the distinctive characteristics and/or history of the Moravians that you noticed being mentioned throughout the story? Did you find any of their practices particularly appealing?

Discussion Guide

Ezekiel's Shadow by David Ryan Long

ISBN 0-7642-2443-3 ⁕ Bethany House

394 pages ⁕ suspense/thriller

The hand of the LORD was upon me, and he brought me out by the Spirit of the LORD and set me in the middle of a valley; it was full of bones that were very dry. . .
Ezek 37:1

This is what the Sovereign LORD says to these bones: I will make breath enter you, and you will come to life . . . Then you will know that I am the LORD.' "
Ezek 37:5

Then he said to me: "Son of man, these bones are the whole house of Israel. They say, 'Our bones are dried up and our hope is gone; we are cut off.'¹² Therefore prophesy and say to them: 'This is what the Sovereign LORD says: O my people, I am going to open your graves and bring you up from them; ¹³ Then you, my people, will know that I am the LORD.¹⁴ I will put my Spirit in you and you will live . . .'"
Ezek 37:11

1. Discuss the title of the book, *Ezekiel's Shadow*, in terms of it's theme and the above scripture (see page 376).

2. Ian says in the story that before his conversion he was only able to see the horror and grief in life, and that his novel, *Hunter*, was his worst expression of that. It was his friend Howard who told him that horror wasn't anything but the fear of death, and the unknown, but that Jesus' death and resurrection had overcome both. Though there is still pain, and suffering, and death in the world, there doesn't need to be any more terror (p. 313). Discuss this, and whether or not you agree, and then discuss what this means in terms of the horror and suffering that was connected to Katherine Jacoby's life (p. 255 & 288). How did her story parallel both Ian's and Howard's (p. 246–255)?

3. Discuss Kevin's reaction to the story of Howard's death (p. 313–314). His definition of horror is when bad things happen to good people (especially people who devoted their lives to service to God), as opposed to pure evil for evil's sake, which is how Ian had formerly seen it. Was Kevin's reaction typical of what many people believe?

4. One of the quotes Ian's stalker uses is from the original draft of his novel *Hunter*, which reads, "The more you change the more likely you are to lose yourself" (p. 255–258). Why is this message so haunting to Ian? Can you recall incidents in the story when this was particularly true for Ian, as well as times when he feared this could never be true for him? Discuss the changes in Ian's life and in his personality since his conversion experience. Also, discuss this in terms of Ian and Rebecca's marriage. What do you think it might have been like before?

5. What do you think people's reaction would be if someone like Stephen King decided to become a Christian? Would we believe that someone who could write stories as twisted and demonically evil as some of his are really change, or would we say something like the woman in the church that Ian and Rebecca visited said about Ian? What reaction do you think the rest of the world would have?

6. Discuss the significance of the scene where Ian faces his editor, Louis Kael (p. 320–323). Why does Louis really want to be "forgiven," and what did you think of Ian's response? Do you think that this was easy for Ian to do based on their former relationship and the trust that was broken? Would you have responded in the same way?

7. *Ezekiel's Shadow* contains quite a few minor characters. Discuss the importance of the Oakley's to this story, as well as the importance of the men in the writer's group, and the role that Trout (Jedidiah) plays in this story.

8. Has this story in any way made you want to take a fresh look at how horror is portrayed in secular books and movies, especially if you are a fan of that particular genre? Explain your response. When would a horror story cross the line and become something you think a Christian shouldn't read? Has our society become desensitized to real horror? What might some real life horrors be?

(Howard's death and the Nazi concentration camps were two types mentioned in this story.)

9. Did you find the ending to this story to be somewhat anticlimactic, or less than credible? Why or why not?

Discussion Guide

Seaside by Terri Blackstock

ISBN 0-310-23318-6 ∾ Zondervan Publishing House
122 pages ∾ a contemporary novella

1. Maggie, a successful photographer, taught her daughters, Corrine and Sarah, a bad lesson that they each carried into their adult lives. However, Maggie tells them while on vacation that the lesson of keeping their promises and fulfilling all their obligations came as a result of anger and bitterness towards their father. She says, "So now we all keep our promises, even if it kills us. We fulfill our obligations, even if they don't make sense . . . none of them really bring any joy" (p. 68). Discuss this in terms of the characters' lives, as well as in the lives of people you know, and maybe even in your own life!

2. What negative lesson do you feel your parents might have taught you that you have carried over into your adult life? What lesson would you like to see your own child(ren) unlearn?

3. One of the themes of this story could be summed up in the hope Maggie feels that she can show her daughters that "time wasted is not always a waste of time" (p. 10). What are some things we might consider to be a waste of time, and how might they really not be? Have you changed your own perspective on what might or might not be a waste of time? Explain.

4. The girls are very jealous of one another's lives (69–71). Corrine is jealous of Sarah's marriage and family, while Sarah is jealous of Corrine's freedom and business savvy, as well as her good looks. However, neither one's life was what it appeared to be from the outside. How true to life is this scenario? Why does the "grass always look greener on the other side," even when we know in reality that it never is? What has your relationship been like with your siblings?

5. Corrine invested in her businesses, while Sarah invested in her church and volunteer organizations, but what they needed to invest in were their souls. And though Maggie had been a life long Christian, she did not teach her daughters this, nor did she learn it herself until the end of her life. What does it mean to invest in your soul, and how can we help each other to do that? How does

our culture work against us doing that? On pages 86–87, Maggie says to her daughters, "I didn't bring you here to get rid of one set of stresses so that you could pick up another one . . . I wanted to remind you where you can find rest. In the Bible we're told that there is a Sabbath rest for the people of God. And . . . we're told not to be anxious, to take our anxieties to the Lord because he cares for us." Why is it difficult for us to find rest and peace in God, and to believe that He knows us intimately and cares about our needs? What in your life do you feel anxious about?

6. Which of these characters did you most relate to and why? What did each of these women decide to do differently in their own lives? Do you feel that the ending was too neatly tied up after only one week on the beach?

7. Corrine misquoted the Bible when she stated, "The Lord helps those who help themselves" (p. 87). Actually, this is a quote from Benjamin Franklin's *Poor Richard's Almanac*. Franklin's *Autobiography* became a moral tract for American students on how to be good and industrial citizens. It not only espoused a strong Puritan work ethic, it encouraged American individualism, and became a road map to wealth. One of his famous 13 Virtues, Industry, states this: "Lose no time; be always employed in something useful; cut off all unnecessary actions." How have we in the twenty-first century, and even in the Church, carried this to the extreme?

8. Discuss Sarah and Corrine's reaction to finding out their mother had cancer, versus their mother's acceptance of it (see chapter 18, 100–104). Why do you think Maggie did not tell her daughters about her cancer until it was too far gone? What did you think about their mother/daughter relationship?

9. Maggie states on page 74 that she had one major regret in her life, and that it was that she had allowed herself to hate the girls' father, and that she had made sure they both knew it . . . And if she could have moved on, their lives might have been different. Discuss regret in terms of being a mother, and also in terms of being a Christian.

Discussion Guide

Winter Passing by Cindy McCormick Martinusen

ISBN 0-7394-1408-9 ❧ Tyndale House Publishers
365 pages ❧ historical novel

"My command is this: Love each other as I have loved you. Greater love hath no man than this, that he lay down his life for his friends."
—Jesus
John 15:12–13

1. Discuss the symbolism in the title of this novel in terms of the passage on page 265: "And only through a winter passing could life be brought to its knees in surrender and prepared for rebirth."

2. What were some of the signs that God was working in Darby's life? How did God work in some of the other characters' lives, especially Brant's, Darby's mother, and her grandmother?

3. The Holocaust was one of the most horrific displays of mankind's potential for evil, and it resulted in many people losing their faith because they could not believe in a God who would let man suffer so much! Brant had apparently talked to Gunther about this, and was remembering Gunther's reply: "Everyone asks how God could allow such a terrible thing. Why does man blame God? For I want to know how *man* could allow such a terrible thing. God gave man dominion over the earth. If we simply can't care for one another or stop evil from breeding and growing—" (p. 180). Discuss both this and Gunther's next comment: "I must believe in God because I've known both evil and love. Evil is easy. Love is hard" (p. 181). What parts of this do you agree or disagree with?

4. When Darby is back in California, she has lunch with her ex fiancé, Derek. She was telling him about Mauthausen, and the interchangeable faces of the SS officers and their victims (see p. 189). Darby tells Derek that she believes "every person on earth is capable of incredible hatred or incredible love. We choose what degree we'll live at" (p. 215). "When we dabble in hatred, selfish pursuits, pride, and contempt for others, our minds can descend without us totally aware, until our actions mirror our mind." Do you agree with her theory? If not, how else would you explain the involve-

ment by so many in the evils of the Holocaust? Also, read Romans 1:18–32 where Paul writes about God's wrath against mankind because of man's wickedness. Many people want to argue that man is not innately evil. What would be your response?

5. Did this story help you to better understand the human weaknesses that caused many to be "converted" by the Nazis? Discuss this especially in terms of the story Bruno Weiler tells Darby, (pages 287–295). He asks Darby for forgiveness. What would be your response? Or, would you rather see them all burn in hell, as was Darby's initial reaction when she was walking through Mauthausen (p. 189)? How many victims do you think were (or are) able to forgive their tormentors? Do you think there is any evil so great that God can't turn it around for good? (Rom. 8:28)

6. Tatianna sacrificed her very life to save her friend's and her friend's unborn child. Do you think that you could have done what she did? Can you imagine ever having to be in that circumstance where you would give up your life for someone not in your immediate family? Do you think it was an effective way to begin the novel with Tatianna's death scene, even though we wouldn't appreciate it until far later in the story, or do you think that scene would have been more powerful coming later?

7. When Darby is in Hallstatt, she meets Grandma Gerringer, an elderly woman who is angry at all Americans because of what she perceives as their arrogant attitude about what happened in Germany and Austria during WWII. She says that they "come to foreign soil and demand answers when they not understand what they asking" (p. 161). She says this after she sees Darby reading *Hitler's Austria*. Discuss what she says, and then what Brant tells her on pages 172–173 about the effects of American culture on Old European culture.

8. One of the lessons that Darby and Brant both learn has to do with living in today, and not in the past, even though you need to learn the truth about the past. What was the biggest lesson you learned from reading this story?

Discussion Guide

Velma Still Cooks in Leeway by Vinita Hampton Wright

ISBN 0805421289 ᴄ⁄ᴐ Broadman & Holman Publishers
295 pages ᴄ⁄ᴐ contemporary fiction

"In the same way, the Spirit helps us in our weakness. We do not know
what we ought to pray for, but the Spirit himself intercedes for us with
groans that words cannot express. And he who searches our hearts knows
the mind of the Spirit, because the Spirit intercedes
for the saints in accordance with God's will."
Romans 8:26

1. This story about life in a small town has some very realistic characters with some very big problems that most Christian fiction does not deal with, thus making the story often unpredictable and edgy. How did this story, with such surprising characters, differ from a story like the *Mitford* series? What particular character did you most feel for, and why? What in this story made you feel the most uncomfortable, and why?

2. Although this story contains a myriad of rich and complex characters, there is a strong theme which runs through it, holding it together like it holds our own lives together, and that is that God can use whatever circumstances we are in, no matter how big or how small, to demonstrate His great love for us so that we may be brought closer to Him. What were the ways God intervened in Velma's life in Leeway, Kansas, and what spiritual lessons did she learn along the way?

3. Velma's spiritual gift is cooking, which she turned into a full-time job after her son was grown and on his own. She went on to spend more than 25 years feeding people, and listening to their stories, and praying over them when she refilled their coffee cups. What can we learn from this story about using our gifts, and about what God can do with any talent if we let Him have it?

4. This story teaches us about love and forgiveness, and several of these characters had huge offenses to forgive! Discuss this especially in terms of Velma, her grandmother (Gran Lenny), and Shellye Pines. What other characters had to learn forgiveness? Who and

what did each one have to forgive, and since it seems that no one gets to escape this spiritual lesson, why do you think it is so important? What happens when we can't forgive?

5. Velma comments throughout her story that she is not good at prayer, and yet she seems to have a lot of faith that whatever kind of prayer she prays it will be received by God, even the ones she does not consciously offer up. In what ways did this novel demonstrate the significance of prayer? In what ways did Velma's story help you better understand what it is to have a life of prayer, as well as the feelings of frustrations and inadequacy that a person might feel in regards to it?

6. This story also deals with feeling and expressing anger towards God. Gran Lenny was angry with God (p. 160), and stated once "that it takes some folks longer to get mad at God than it does others. But everybody does get there, sooner or later" (p. 234). Velma recalled how that sounded awful to her when she was young, but real anger rose in her spirit when she thought about how "Doris's problems were much bigger than the effects of an act of sin here or there" (p. 235). Do you sometimes feel this way about people you know? Discuss this in terms of how we often view God's lack of intervention in our lives. What *blessings* in Velma's life reinforced her trust in God?

7. This story is also about having hope in the Resurrection. After reading this story, what might you say to people who suffer like these characters, that would offer them not just the *belief* in a resurrection, but the *hope* that when we die it will be different than just "living better than before" (p. 235 & 272)? What do you think Doris meant when she said this? Paul tells us that we need to have faith, hope, and love. Do you agree with Velma that the church oftentimes neglects *hope*? (Read I Peter 3:15, I Peter 1:3–7, Romans 5:1–5, Romans 12:12–13)

8. Part of what makes this novel so moving is that it is told in first person through Velma's eyes, and in her voice. What, in your opinion, made Velma seem like such a likeable and reliable narrator? What effect did the ending have on your feelings about her and the story?

Discussion Guide

The Immortal by Angela Elwell Hunt
ISBN 0-8488-1630-5 ❧ Word Publishing
385 pages ❧ contemporary novel/parable

"You diligently study the Scriptures because you think that by them you possess eternal life. These are the Scriptures that testify about me, yet you refuse to come to me to have life."
—Jesus
John 5:39–40

1. What would you expect a Christian who had lived two thousand years to be like in terms of his life? Do you think you would improve if given that long to live? What do you think you would find to do for 2,000 years? Do you believe you could stay faithful through that many lives? Did this story make you feel any different about death?

2. Hunt uses the above scripture as a prelude to her story about Asher, the Wandering Jew. What is the significance of this passage to the message in her story? What is the difference between turning to Scripture and turning to Christ? How can a person diligently study the Scriptures and not turn to Christ? What does it take to turn to Christ?

3. This is a very strong story about the message of God's grace. It takes a brand new Christian to make a two thousand year old man finally understand that he cannot earn God's forgiveness. The key is when Claudia tells Asher that he never trusted Christ for his salvation, and that God, in His mercy, might have given Asher all this time to turn from his sin! (see pages 360–361). Asher believed that his sin was so horrible that he was doomed to pay for it until Christ's return. Do we sometimes feel this way about our own sins? Also, are there times when we might wish this burden of guilt onto other people?

4. Discuss the turning point in Claudia's life when she was weighing her decision to become a believer in Christ (p. 324–328). What kind of examples did those around her who were Christian set, that is, what influence did they have on her life? Do you think

that once she accepted Christ she could continue in her old life? Explain. How might Claudia use her gift of "reading" people to serve Christ?

5. Discuss the statement Asher makes when he says, "God is not *fair*. He is *just*. There is a difference" (p. 290). What difference does it make when we insist on seeing God as Claudia does, when after hearing Asher's story about losing his wife, she says: "It just doesn't seem fair. And if God is anything, he should be fair." What might it be in our own lives that causes us to get angry at God because we feel like he isn't being fair?

6. Reverend Synn, or Il Direttore, espouses what many non-Christians believe to be the summation of the message of Jesus: "[E]nlightenment must come from within a man or a woman. When we look for God and giftedness in ourselves, we invariably find it . . . You will find God if you take time to meditate on his love and beauty" (p. 267). He goes on to deliver a very fine oratorio about everyday miracles, peace, and love, which all sound very good: "Peace and contentment are found through the simplicity of truth—in living authentically, simply, peacefully. Seek the peaceful life, and you will find it" (p. 269). This is a very popular belief held by many good people who want to put Jesus in the same category as all other spiritual teachers. What would be your explanation to someone who said this to you?

7. What did you feel were some of the strengths of this story? The weaknesses? What made this story's conflict concerning the Antichrist different from other stories you might have read on the same subject?

8. What is the difference between believing in grace and living it (see page 362)? Ephesians 2:4–5 "But because of his great love for us, God, who is rich in mercy, made us alive with Christ even when we were dead in transgression, and it is by grace you have been saved." verses 8–9 "For it is by grace you have been saved, through faith, and this is not from yourselves, it is a gift of God, not by works, so that no one can boast." How many different ways did Asher try to earn his salvation? On what did he base this belief?

Discussion Guide

One Shenandoah Winter by T. Davis Bunn

ISBN 0-7852-7217-8 ∽ Thomas Nelson Publishers
265 pages ∽ holiday fiction

1. What did you find most memorable about this story? What role do you feel the setting (1961, small town life in the Shenandoah Mountains) made on the story?

2. One of the most moving storylines in this novella has to do with what Poppa Joe's living and death taught everyone. Even after the funeral, no one felt sadness; instead they felt their own spirits had undergone a healing. Why do you think this is so? Discuss what most moved you about the meaning Poppa Joe gave to life, and to the dignity he gave to death (p. 91, 174–175). Did you experience any type of healing as you read this story?

3. Rev. Brian Blackstone's Christmas Eve sermon had to do with Faith, with taking our hands off the controls and letting God have them, of releasing the impossibilities of our human frailties over to God. He says that it is fear that keeps us from doing this (p. 218–221). It was Nathan who took this sermon to heart and let go of his desire as a doctor to control the healing of his young cancer patients, but Connie had some lessons to learn herself. What form did her controlling nature take? What were some of the results? Why did Rev. Brian say that it was hard to reach a person like her (p. 179)? Do you think he would say that about you? What lesson did you take from this sermon? (Read Hebrews chapter 11 for a definition of faith)

4. Connie often felt lonely, unhappy, unsuccessful, and angry (p. 8–9, 42, 65), yet she was by all accounts, a good Christian. We know God does not want us to feel and live like this, so how does it happen? Explain it in terms of Connie's life, then in terms of your own life. What had to happen for Connie to change, and what had to happen for you to change (and hopefully you have!)? Could Connie have spent her life righteously justifying her anger, and thus never reaping the joy God had planned for her life?

5. Poppa Joe said about Nathan that he needed to find his strength and his purpose (p.181 & 254). What were the outward changes

that demonstrated to the rest of the world that he had indeed done both of those?

6. This is a story not only about death, and acceptance of it, but of life, and acceptance of it as well. Back to Rev. Blackstone's sermon: "We celebrate here tonight [Christmas Eve] the conquest of fear . . . Fear is vanquished! Death is conquered! . . . To all who suffer and worry and hurt and know fear, our Savior says, 'Come! Come and I will give you rest! Come and drink the cup of eternal healing! Come and sing at the holy feast of life! Come and celebrate! Why? Because, I your King, have conquered death. I, your King, have conquered fear!'" Christ was born for one purpose, and that was to die for us and our sins so that we may have life, and have it abundantly! (p. 221). Discuss how some of the characters in this story were "singing at the holy feast of life." What burden do you need to hand over to God so that you too may "sing at the holy feast of life this Christmas season?"

Bonus Reader's Guides

1. *The Heart Reader* by Terri Blackstock

It is the story of a man, Sam Bennett, who wakes up one morning, and after having a strange dream based on the story of the lost coin and the lost sheep in Luke 15, is able to hear the voices of people all around him. He can look at them and hear their deepest spiritual needs, only their lips aren't moving and they don't' seem to know they've said anything at all. Working with his pastor John, his own life begins to change.

2. *Saint Maybe* by Anne Tyler

Set in 1965, the Bedloe family is living a happy existence in Baltimore, until a single tragic event changes their lives forever. Seventeen-year-old Ian Bedloe blames himself for the sudden accidental death of his older brother, and is almost crushed by the unbearable weight of secret guilt over something he had said to him. Then one January evening he catches sight of the neon sign of the Church of the Second Chance. Believing that the brand of Christianity his family church offers can never cover his sins, he enters here and discovers that he must learn to bear the burden of sacrifice and love that God has placed on him.

3. *Daughter of China* by C. Hope Flinchbaugh

Mei Ling longs for an education, a career, and love, but the political system she lives under does not tolerate religious belief. This is a story of the persecuted church in China, and one young woman's refusal to give up her faith, even when it means undergoing severe beatings and imprisonment. Woven throughout the story is the issues of ancestor worship, and the one-child law, which has resulted in baby killings and abortions.

4. *Perelandra* by C. S. Lewis

This is the second book in the Space Trilogy, which continues the adventures of Dr. Ransom, who must struggle against the Devil to save Perelandra from the same fate that Earth underwent when Eve succumbed to Satan. This story will shed light on the very few verses in Genesis that mentions the Garden of Eden and the fall of mankind. How long might it have taken to teach Eve the concepts of vanity, discomfort, duty, self-sacrifice, courage, and even excitement? What is the knowledge of evil but maybe the conscious awareness of self and the desire to fulfill our own wants, so that we disobey God? In a land of innocence, splendor, and unsullied peace, what might it have taken to encourage free will, and then disobedience to perfect Love?

5. *The Tao of Pooh* by Benjamin Hoff

This is a humorous look at what it means to follow the way of Pooh, or rather to develop the childlike simplicity, effortless action, and spontaneity that defines the very nature of A. A. Milne's beloved Winnie-the-Pooh. Hoff also examines the negative nature of Eeyore, the hesitant nature of Piglet, the calculating, busybody nature of Rabbit, and the egotistical, pontificating nature of Owl. It's also about learning what your limitations are and working with them, instead of letting them work against you.

6. *The Red Tent* by Anita Daimont

Told by Dinah, the eleventh child and only daughter of Jacob, it is a story about her father, and her mothers, Leah, Rachel, Zilpah, and Bilhal, the four wives of Jacob. It reveals the traditions of womanhood in ancient Hebrew times, and the world of the red tent, where the women celebrate their monthly cycles; they whisper stories and secrets, and share days of rest from their toil in the glaring sun. The tent is also the place where each woman gives birth to new life. While Daimont greatly embellishes on the biblical version of the story, she offers authentic details about history, geography, religion, superstition, food, dress, lodging, family rituals, manners, and the medical practices of life lived among sheep and goats. Speaking for the first time in over 3,000 years, Dinah begins by telling her mothers' stories, then she tells her own stories, then she looks at her life in Egypt where she flees after facing the violence in Shechem, which left her a young widow. This is merely a what-if scenario presented by Daimont. This novel has attracted much controversy, but managed to make its way to the bestseller list by word of mouth.

7. *Gift From the Sea* by Anne Morrow Lindbergh

A modern day classic, it's a book of meditations on youth and age, love and marriage, solitude, peace, and contentment. Shedding the shell of her life, Anne writes a group of spiritual reflections during a brief vacation by the ocean on how to get more in tune with the rhythm of the sea and find more creative pauses.

Discussion Guide

The Heart Reader by Terri Blackstock

ISBN 0-8499-1651-8 ☙ Word Publishing
137 pages ☙ novella

1. Is Sam Bennett's initial reaction to his spiritual gift typical of what most people might feel if given the same ability to read people's hearts? He feels he is not the right person for the job (p. 23) Why did Sam feel he was inadequate for the job? What exactly scared him about his gift (p. 27–29 & 62)? Can you think of other servants of God who felt that they were not the right person for the job God was telling them to do?

2. What would you do if you actually knew the spiritual needs of everyone you came in contact with? What were some of the needs of the different people in this story, and do you think those needs are probably true to life? Just considering some of the people that you know, what are some other needs? Do you agree with Sam's conclusion concerning the difference between the needs of non-Christians and the needs of Christians (p. 133)?

3. Do you think God hears the cries from people's hearts differently than we do? Do you think we are always honest with ourselves about what our own needs are? Explain. (See pages 41, 68, & 89)

4. Pastor John says that most people can't hear with the ears they've got, that people's ears are clogged up and that we can't hear the most obvious things (p. 3). What does he mean, and do you agree with that or not? On what do you base your response?

5. What does Kate mean when she says, "I keep thinking that I need God to break my heart so I can get back in tune with him (p. 65)?

6. Do you agree with Sam's new conviction that helping our Christian friends spiritually, and hoping that we influence people with the examples we set in our lives is *not* enough (p. 80–81)?

7. Discuss the reaction of the Chairman of the deacons, Lawrence Shipman, to the influx of new converts to their church (p. 107). Do you think his would be a typical or an atypical response in your church, or any other church? Also, see page 42 where John voices his complaint about being a preacher. Does what he say ring true in your church?

8. Do you think any of us would behave differently if we were really convicted "That there's a hell and it's real and [that] people are going there" (p. 83)? Discuss this in terms of Annabelle York's worry as she lay on her deathbed in the hospital (p. 46).

9. The list of places where Sam heard the spiritual cries of people is quite diverse: in the diner, on the street, in the elevator, in the supermarket, at his work, in the hospital, at the ball game, in Shoney's, and at the bus station. Name just one place that you go during your daily routine that it might be possible if you really listened to hear the needy cry of even one soul.

10. Discuss the problem of inferiority that Sally, Sam's secretary, seemed to be suffering. Does it surprise you that Christians like Sally describes herself as being could have missed or forgotten the message of Christ's love, and the meaning of Luke 15 (the parables of the lost coin, the lost sheep, and the lost son)?

11. How did Sam change as a Christian once he got used to his gift, and then after it left him?

12. The last four sentences in the story pretty much sums up its message: "And what he couldn't hear, the Holy Spirit could. *He could do what Sam couldn't* (emphasis is mine). This man needed Jesus Christ. That was all he [Sam] needed to know." Did anything about this story's message inspire you or bother you?

Discussion Guide

Saint Maybe[1] by Anne Tyler

ISBN 0-449-91160-8 ❧ Fawcett Columbine/Ballentine Books
337 pages ❧ *NY Times* Bestseller

"Blessed are those who mourn, for they shall be comforted."
Matthew 5:4

1. Discuss how gossip (misunderstanding what we see; thoughtlessly spoken words) played a role in the downfall of the Bedloe family. Do you think Danny's accident was Ian's fault?

2. Ian always seemed to be trying to define himself. Who am I? Am I a sinner, or am I a saint? (Saint Maybe was a term Daphne coined as she yelled at Ian that she was not like him. p. 264) Discuss the significance of the title *Saint Maybe* as it applied to Ian's life and his attitude of self-loathing.

3. Although the Bedloes considered themselves to be Christian (they attended Dober Street Presbyterian p. 127), Ian felt that in terms of the sins he had committed, their brand of Christianity was not enough. How was the Church of the Second Chance different, and how did it offer Ian a 2nd chance? Discuss the Church in terms of both its spirituality and its legalisms. (Also, see p. 124 as one explanation for the religion of the Second Chance, citing I John 3:18 "Let us not love in word, neither in tongue, but in deed and in truth.") Do you think Anne Tyler portrayed religious fundamentalists in a true and/or positive light? (Also see Holy House of the Gospel on p. 186)

4. Life doesn't always seem fair, and Ian often did not want to carry the burden that he had put upon him. At times he even struggled with the idea that he was wasting his life. Finally, Rev. Emmett said to him, "This is your life. Live it." Do you think that was wise advice? (p. 213)

5. Ian had several spiritual struggles, and one of them was that he saw his burden of raising the children as being a punishment from God. Rev. Emmett saw the children not as Ian's burden, but as his joy. He

---

1. This book contains some offensive language.

went on to explain to Ian that his burden was not in his waiting to be forgiven by God, but for himself to forgive his brother and sister-in-law. Why do you think Emmett said this to Ian? (p. 225)

6. How well do you think Anne Tyler captured family life in this novel? Explain. What effect did placing this story in the 1960s have on the plot (for example: family values, gender roles, etc.)?

7. Anne Tyler is known for creating peculiar yet lovable characters, and there are a host of them in this novel. Who was your favorite, and why? (Danny, Lucy, Thomas, Agatha, Daphne, Rev. Emmett, Mr. and Mrs. Bedloe, *et al.*)

8. How do you think Ian's life would have turned out had he not had to raise three children? What sacrifices did he have to make? Did you see any alternative to Ian having to raise those kids on his own? Did you like the way Anne Tyler wrote the ending of this story? Why?

Discussion Guide

Daughter of China by C. Hope Flinchbaugh

ISBN 0-7642-2731-9 ✆ Bethany House Publishers
278 pages ✆ contemporary Christian fiction

"Therefore, I urge you, brothers, in view of God's mercy, to offer your bodies as living sacrifices, holy and pleasing to God—this is your spiritual act of worship."
Rom 12:1

"This third I will bring into the fire; I will refine them like silver and test them like gold. They will call on my name and I will answer them; I will say, 'They are my people,' and they will say, 'The LORD is our God.'"
Zech 13:9

1. After having delved into the world of the persecuted church, how did reading this book change the way you saw your own position and involvement in the church? Do you think that we take our freedom to worship too much for granted? Discuss some of the testimonies given by the people in the story.

2. Do you think you could be brave in declaring your Christianity if you knew that it might mean your death? What if it meant a very slow torture before dying?

3. After having been severely beaten in prison, Mei Lin Kwan is still able to sing praises to God. One song that she sings is *I Surrender All*. What did that mean to her in her situation? What does that mean to you in yours? Make a list of what you could surrender to God. Make a list of what you can't. Which is longer?

4. What did you learn about Chinese religion in terms of ancestor worship (back to 7 generations), fortune telling and divination, and Buddhism? How does religion still play a role in Chinese society even after it has been outlawed? Discuss why you think it might be hard for Amah (Mei Lin's grandmother) to convert to Christianity. Why would a communist regime need to stamp out all religion?

5. Woven throughout this story is the issue of the one-child law, which has resulted in baby killings and abortions. Before reading this book, did you know there was such a law? Discuss this in terms of what it means for people in China. What did Fei Gong mean when she said that "Satan hates babies?" (p. 253).

6. Mei Lin expressed her hatred for communist governments, believing that in a free democratic country something as horrible as baby killing would never exist. Pastor Wong tells Mei Lin that no form of government can change a person's heart, that only Jesus can do this; and, that sin exists everywhere under every form of government (p. 253). Discuss what he meant by this.

7. In this story Christians are viewed as being counter revolutionaries, and Bibles are counted as contraband. How does this affect their daily lives (in terms of schooling, house-church meetings, dating)?

8. Over and over, the people in this story refer to "the God who blesses," and "a God who is faithful." Do you think that if you were in their shoes you would be more able or less able to see God's blessings and faithfulness? Explain.

9. Discuss the importance to the characters in this book of memorizing scriptures and hymns.

Discussion Guide

Perelandra by C. S. Lewis

ISBN 0-684-82382-9 ∽ Scribner Paperback/Simon & Schuster
222 pages ∽ science fiction

1. In what way, if any, did reading this story shed light on the Biblical account of Adam and Eve in the Garden of Eden? In what way(s) did it cause you to stretch your imagination? In what way(s) did it upset you?

2. The first six chapters of this book deal with the setting, mostly of Perelandra (its innocence, its splendor, and its unsullied peace). What do you think is the significance of spending so much time on this one element? Discuss the darkness and fear that Lewis describes on his way to see Ransom, and the mention of spiritual warfare versus physical warfare against evil (p. 24 & 143).

3. What ideas did Lewis take from Genesis chapters 1–3 and incorporate into his own story? How do the two stories parallel each other, and how do they differ?

4. Discuss Lewis' portrayal of the devil in this work. (See particularly pages 108–111, 128, 146, and 153.) Discuss how the Un-Man tried to talk The Lady of Perelandra into disobeying God's order not to sleep or spend the night on the Fixed Land, and compare this with what we know in the Genesis account. How does this harmonize with the themes of human freedom, choice, goodness, and obedience to the will of God? (See pages 69–70, 74–75, 97, 118, 129, 142, 204, & 208.)

5. Adam and Eve were given dominion over all the animals, as were The Lady and King of Perelandra. Discuss how this is portrayed in Lewis's fictional Paradise. (See pages 65 and 211.)

6. What did it mean in Lewis's Paradise to have knowledge of good and evil? Cite some specific examples from this story. (See especially pages 114, 126, and 135–139.)

7. Lewis's story also includes the eldilas, or angels. In what way(s) does this challenge what you might have previously thought about how angels serve God and man (195–196)?

8. Would it bother you to think that God as the Great Creator might have created other worlds besides ours, either before our own or

after our own? Discuss what Lewis says about this in terms of Perelandra (p. 213–218). Discuss what you think is meant by "the Great Dance," beginning on page 213 and continuing to page 219. Discuss Lewis's idea of God never repeating a single thing in creation. Does reading *Perelandra* help you to better grasp that idea?

9. Discuss what might have happened had Adam and Eve not sinned. Would Satan have been allowed to tempt them forever? How would God have stopped it? (Ransom wonders this on page 145.)

10. Discuss the symbolism of the name "Ransom" and what is said about there not being a second crucifixion, or maybe not even a second Incarnation (p. 148–149).

Discussion Guide

The Tao of Pooh, by Benjamin Hoff

ISBN 0-14-006747-7 ✑ Penguin Books

158 pages ✑ Humor

"He should become a fool so that he may become wise."
I Corinthians 3:18

"Unless you change and become like little children,
you will never enter the kingdom of heaven."
Matthew 18:3

"Jesus answered, "I am the way . . ."
John 14:6

1. The key principles are Taoism are: Natural Simplicity, Effortless Action, Spontaneity, and Compassion. The symbol of Taoism is flowing water. How might these concepts have their counterparts in Christianity?

2. What is the difference between childlikeness, and childishness? Which is Pooh more like? Explain the principle of the uncarved block (p. 18–21) using Pooh as an example. Include with this a discussion of Wu Wei, or the Pooh Way (p. 67–88).

3. Discuss the concept of Inner Nature (p. 38–65), using Tigger as an example. Do you know anyone who is like that?

4. Discuss the Bisy Backson (p. 93–112), using Rabbit as an example. Do you know anyone who is like that? Discuss our cultural myths of the Great Reward and Saving Time (p. 112).

5. Since "doing" denotes action, explain the concept of Doing Nothing (p. 141–143, 158). Have you ever been able to do nothing?

6. Explain the Taoist concept of Wisdom (p. 149–151). How does this differ from the "wise" image of Owl? Discuss the Biblical definition, and then the world's definition.

7. Joseph Campbell, in writing about the Hero's Journey, defined the first stage of the journey as "birth," or as starting out as a fool. The

role of the fool represents innocence, or a childlike nature. The fool also represents starting out on a new stage of life. It stands for adventure and openness to new experiences. It flirts with possibilities, and holds out hope, promise, and desire. It represents a willingness to risk the loss of what you have been, and grow to what you can become. Discuss this definition, and then apply it to I Cor. 3:18. How does it differ from the stereotypical definition? (Proverbs and Ecclesiastes have much to say on being a fool.) What persons in our history were initially perceived as fools and why? What persons were actually foolish?

8. Explain the difference between a fool and a wise man using Pooh and Owl in your examples.

9. Briefly describe the following characters and explain how their personality types are represented in our culture: Pooh, Piglet, Eeyore, Owl, Rabbit, and Tigger. (Examples: gloomy, pessimistic Eeyore; intellectual Owl; impulsive Tigger; etc.)

Discussion Guide

The Red Tent[2] by Anita Diamant

ISBN 0-312-19551-6 ⌗ Picador USA/St. Martin's Press
321 pages ⌗ Biblical Romance (*NY Times* Bestseller)

1. Read Genesis 34 and discuss how reading *The Red Tent* effects your perspective on Dinah's story and also on the story of Jacob, which precedes it, and of Joseph that follows. (To read the entire story, begin in Genesis 27 where Jacob receives Isaac's blessing, and read through to the end of Genesis 50 to Joseph's death.) Does *The Red Tent* raise questions about other men and women in the Bible? How does Diamant's story compare with other women of the Bible whose stories have been written and published by Christian publishing houses?

2. Polygamy is a double-edged sword. Discuss the marital dynamics of Jacob to each of his four wives. Compare his relationship with each woman. What do you make of the relationships among the wives to each other? What are some of the positives, and some of the negatives?

3. Discuss the differences or similarities in Dinah's relationship with each of her "mothers."

4. Daimant strives to portray the women not as victims but as active agents in their own lives. How do you see both Leah and Rachel in this light? How does Daimant twist the biblical story so that the women have more power than the men?

5. Discuss Dinah's twelve brothers. Discuss their relationships with each other, with Dinah, and with Jacob and his wives. How does Dinah get treated differently as the only daughter?

6. Discuss the issues of fertility, childbearing, and childbirth as they are exemplified in *The Red Tent*. How do they differ from current day practices? How are they similar? Do you believe it was possible that Jacob would not have known about the women's fertility gods?

7. What do you think of this culture in which the Feminine has not yet been totally divorced from the Divine, and in which Goddesses are venerated along with gods? Discuss how Daimant uses the women's religion as a way to unify and support the women's lives,

2. This book contains some material that may be offensive.

which are completely separate from the men's. How does El, the God of Abraham, Isaac, and Jacob, fit into this? Do you believe that in a patriarchal society it's possible that men might not have provided religious instruction to their wives? What were some particular spiritual concerns of the women?

8. The most shocking character is Rebecca. Anyone familiar with the biblical account of Rebecca as being one of scripture's classic matriarchs may be surprised to see her portrayed so harshly. Why might Daimant paint her as such an unsympathetic character? Discuss this as an issue of the potential negative side of female power.

9. Discuss how Dinah changes and matures as she grows from childhood to old age. Is Shalem and Dinah's love affair believable based on the biblical account of her rape? How likely is it that Dinah would have been allowed to walk around, on her own, unprotected? Discuss her relationship with Benia. What lessons does she learn from life?

10. The story is told from Dinah's point of view. How does this effect how the reader sees the men? How would the story be different if told from Jacob's point of view? Do you think there is a bias that favors men's stories and downplays most women's stories in the bible? Explain.

Appendix A[1]

Great Website Addresses for the Christian Reader

Great Web Sites for Ordering Books

www.Amazon.com

The largest on-line bookseller; full product line; charges a $1.00 per item fee on top of shipping & handling; a good way to view book covers and read excerpts about the books.

www.Barnes & Noble.com

Largest U.S. chain bookseller; charges a $1.00 per item fee on top of shipping & handling; view book covers and read excerpts about the books.

www.bestbookbuys.com

Searches other booksellers; free.

www.bookfinder.com

The #1 free on-line book directory in the world; will search 20,000 booksellers around the world to find new, used, out of print, rare, and signed books; not only is it comprehensive, but is easy to use.

1BookStreet.com

Discount bookseller; free shipping; may browse other book streets like 1JesusWay.com which contains Christian book titles.

---

1. A non-comprehensive list of web addresses for ordering books on-line, reviews, discussions, and author information.

www.christianbook.com

$5.00 yearly membership fee; will send you a catalog; very low prices; will ship regular mail between 24-48 hours; shipping and handling fee up to $20.00 is $3.50, $20.01-$50.00 is $5.00, and $50.01-$100 is 10%, and over $100.00 is 8%; no extra per item fee. Toll-free number for orders is 1-888-247-2665.

www.ChristianKingdom.com

An on-line Christian bookstore which carries a full line of products; fiction titles must be searched by key word; no per item fee, but UPS ground shipping charges are high; may call toll free at 1-877-We-Filter.

www.dealtime.com

Searches other booksellers; free.

www.ecampus.com

A mega college bookstore, includes textbooks, nonfiction, and fiction titles, all discounted; free shipping of purchases over $35.00; no per item fee.

www.Half.com

A site to buy used books, and sell your old ones.

www.interlinkbooks.com

A site to find new international and world fiction, travel books, poetry, cook books, and books of political and historical interest. You can request a free catalog; they also have a toll free number: 1-800-238-LINK.

www.varsitybooks.com

Sells any book that has been used as a textbook at a college or university in the U.S., as well as bestsellers; UPS ground shipping is $4.95; no per item fee.

Recommended Magazines for the Reading Life

Today's Christian Woman

www.TodaysChristianWoman.net; cover price is $3.95, subscription price is $17.95 for 6 issues; call 1-800-365-9484 to subscribe; besides great articles, it also includes book reviews, titles by new authors, and a Christian fiction bestseller list.

Book

www.bookmagazine.com; cover price is $4.95 per issue; subscription price is $20.00 for 6 issues; call 1-800-317-book; feature stories, articles, book and poetry reviews, best of lists.

The New York Times Book Review

www.nytimes.com; pages and pages of reviews, best seller lists, publisher's ads, and special editions.

"Reading Woman"

A quarterly newsletter containing short reviews and excerpts from works of fiction and nonfiction by both men and women; contact "Reading Woman"/P.O. Box 19116/Minneapolis, MN, 55419/or, www.reading-woman.com.

"Reading Women"

A newsletter of literary criticism for reading groups; $29.00 subscription; send your name and address to: Reading Women/P.O. Box 296/Winnetka, IL 60093.

Order Free Reading Group Guides[2]

www.penguinputnam.com

Also you can call the Marketing Department at 1-800-778-6425 for additional copies.

---

2. These contain descriptions of the books, author biographies, and suggestions for further reading.

www.randomhouse.com/vintage/read

Also you can call 1-800-793-BOOK.

www.readinggroupguides.com

This website contains Reader's Guides to hundreds of books, with new books listed on the home page. Books can be searched by title or by author, or they may be searched by category, including one labeled Christian, which has 24 titles.

www.vintagebooks.com

Free group guides, excerpts, author interviews, online discussions, and more.

www.sourcebooks.com

Also you can call 630-961-3900.

www.perennialclassics.com

Also you can call 1-800-242-7737.

www.harpercollins.com/readers

Also you can call 1-800-242-7737.

Other Great Resources and Web Addresses

Bartleby.com

An internet publisher of literary classics, nonfiction, verse, and reference books; free of charge; for the home, classroom, and desktop; full-text on line.

www.BookBrowse.com

Read book excerpts from current bestsellers, and other recently published books, both fiction and nonfiction; plus reviews, summaries, and author biographies.

www.bookreporter.com

Discover books, authors, readers, and much more.

BookTalk

1-800-authors; listen to authors discussing their books; just dial toll-free, punch in the code of the book you want to hear about, punch again, and you can buy the book, or any other title, over the phone. Some examples: *How Reading Changed My Life*, by Anna Quindlen #4722; *Saving Faith*, by David Baldacci #4212; and *Tuesdays With Morrie*, by Mitch Albom #1222.

www.cli-nc.org (Christian International Library)

Go online to find out how you can donate your used Christian books to Christian Library International, an organization that distributes them to prisons, shelters, and international missions.

www.netLibrary.com

The most comprehensive collection of on-line books and resource materials; you may search every word in the entire collection, as well as search within a particular book; contains thousands of full-text titles; check out is free; when check out time expires, your eBooks are automatically returned to the netLibrary.

www.oprah.com

For a list of all of her book club selections.

www.questia.com

An independent e-library which aims to offer an on-line database of 250,000 books to scholars and students for an affordable subscription fee.

www.recordedbooks.com

Unabridged audios on cassette and CD, call 1-800-638-1304; thousands of titles available in an easy rent-by-mail system; preaddressed, pre-stamped boxes make returns easy.

Appendix B[3]

A Glossary of Literary Terms

allegory: A narrative in which the agents and actions, and sometimes the setting as well, are contrived so as to make sense on the literal level, and to make sense on the conceptual level. There are two main types of allegory: (1) Historical and political allegory, and (2) the allegory of ideas, in which the literal characters represent abstract concepts, and the plot incorporates and exemplifies a doctrine or thesis. Both types of allegory may either be sustained throughout a work, as in John Bunyan's *Pilgrim Progress* (1678), or else serve merely as an episode in a nonallegorical work. The central device in the second type, the sustained allegory of ideas, is the personification of abstract entities such as virtues, vices, states of mind, modes of life, and types of character; in the more explicit allegories, such reference is specified by the names given to characters and places. *Hind's Feet on High Places* is a moral and religious allegory in prose narrative. Special types of allegory include the fable, the beast fable, and the parable.

allusion: A reference, either explicit or indirect, in a literary work to a well-known person, place, or event in history, the Bible, literature, or mythology.

ambiguity: Story, language, and action that evoke conflicting meanings and convey diverse attitudes and feelings.

analogy: The comparison of one object, condition, process, or event to another in order to clarify or intensify the image or thought.

antihero: A protagonist who is distinguished from the classical hero by his or her flaws and inability to perform heroic deeds. Traditionally, heroes were of a special status, such as kings, noblemen, or princes who distinguished themselves with courage, abilities, and noble deeds; ordinary men were designated as anti-heroes.

antagonist: A character in a story who stands in opposition to the hero (*see* Protagonist). The conflict between the antagonist and protagonist often generates the action or plot of the story.

---

3. I put these here to help you to have better literary discussions. These are not only definitions of literary terms, but can be used as possible points of book discussions.

apologetics: The oral or written defense of something. For example, theologians use the term *Christian apologetics*, which is the defense of Christianity.

autobiography: An account of a person's life written by that person. It is to be distinguished from the memoir—in which the emphasis is not on the autho'r developing self, but on the people the author has known and witnessed—and from the private diary or journal, which is a day-to-day record of the events in a person's life, written for personal use and pleasure, with little or no thought of publication. The first fully developed autobiography is also one of the greatest: The *Confessions* of St. Augustine, written in the 4th century. The design of this profound and subtle spiritual autobiography center's on the author's mental crisis and a recovery in which he discovers his Christian identity and religious vocation. Calvinism. A doctrine put forth by John Calvin in his famous work titled *The Institutes of the Christian Religion* and the "Bay Psalm Book" (1640). He emphasized predestination, and strict discipline.

character: A person in a literary work, sometimes classified as either *flat* (quickly describable, and not typically developed, or non-changing), or *round* (more developed, complex).

climax: The point of the highest interest and intensity in the plot.

colloquial: Having to do with ordinary, informal speech.

conflict: Interaction that creates tension in a story, either between two characters, or between a character and values, doctrines, time, place, or nature. Traditionalists consider conflict to be paramount to a story, to be that which keeps a plot moving.

convention: A traditional or accepted way of doing or expressing something.

credibility: In reference to a work of literature, it is how believable any part of a story line is. An example might be over how believable a character's response is to something that has been said, or something that has happened in the story. Some stories ask us to suspend our disbelief from beginning to end so that the story's credibility lies within its own set of rules for form, like in a fairy story, but other stories are set up to reflect real life, and their flaw is that they ask the readers to believe too much.

dialect: The speech of a particular region or class.

dialogue: The exchange of words between characters.

dystopia: Literally, it means a "bad place," or the opposite of utopia, which represents an ideal, non-existent political state and way of life. Dystopian novels represent a dark reality, or a very unpleasant imaginary world, in which ominous tendencies of our present social, political, and technological order are projected in some future culmination.

elegy: A long and formal poem meditating on, or lamenting, the dead.

epic: An extended narrative poem, written in an elevated style, recounting the deeds of a legendary or actual hero.

epiphany: In a religious sense, a "manifestation" that signifies God's presence. In a secular experience, an epiphany occurs when a character has a sense of revelation, an enlightenment—one of those moments when troubling things become clarified or events in life become connected in a new revelatory way.

farce: A type of comedy, usually satiric, that relies on exaggerated character types, ridiculous situations, and often, horseplay.

feminism: Attention to topics and themes of particular concern to women, frequently emphasizing injustices.

genteel: Overly polite and seeking to avoid any possibly offensive language or topics.

genre: A term used to indicate the various categories in which literary works are grouped by form; derived from the French word for kind or type.

gothic novel: A type of novel, first popularized in the late eighteenth century, characterized by thrill-provoking and supernatural events.

grotesque: When applied to literature, the word has come to denote characters who are spiritually or physically deformed.

imagery: A term used frequently in literary criticism to refer either to figures of speech or verbal representations of sensory objects or sensations intended to evoke specific visceral and emotional reactions.

interior monologue: A technique used in the writing of a novel or short story to record the inner thoughts and emotional responses of a character; also called stream of consciousness.

irony: A rhetorical device in which the author conveys a meaning opposite to the words actually used.

juxtapose: To place words or images close to one another, frequently for ironic purposes.

local color: Picturesque and idiosyncratic detail about a particular region or location.

melodrama: Although the term literally means "a play with music," today it denotes a play with stereotyped characters and highly charged emotions, usually with a romantic plot and a happy ending.

metaphor: A figure of speech implying a comparison between objects of different classes or categories by saying one object *is* another, not *like* another, which is called simile.

miracle play: A type of drama, common in medieval England, that depicts a miracle performed by a saint, or an incident in the life of one. These plays are not usually based strictly on scriptural accounts.

mock epic: A long poem, intended to be humorous, that treats a trivial subject in the lofted, exalted style of the epic poem.

morality play: A type of drama, popular in medieval England, characterized by a pronounced use of allegory to point up a moral teaching.

mood: The atmosphere or general feeling of a work.

motif: An element—a type of incident, device, reference, or formula—which recurs frequently in literature.

mystery play: A type of medieval play based on Biblical stories.

myth: In classical Greek, "mythos" signified any story or plot, whether true or invented. A myth is one story in a mythology—a system of hereditary stories which were once believed to be true by a particular cultural group, and which served to explain (in terms of the intentions and actions of supernatural beings) why the world is as it is, and why things happen as they do, as well as to establish the rationale for social customs and observances, and the sanctions for the rules by which people conduct their lives.

naturalism: A type of realistic fiction that developed in the late nineteenth century. It presupposes that human beings are like puppets, controlled completely by external and internal forces.

orthodox: Generally approved or accepted.

oxymoron: Literally means "acutely silly." A figure of speech in which contradictory ideas are combined to create a condensed paradox: *sweet sorrow, wise fool.*

parable: A story or short narrative told in order to imply an analogy between it and a lesson, or moral point, that the storyteller is trying to make. The parable was one of Jesus' favorite devices as a teacher.

pastoral: A poem about shepherds and rural life, derived from ancient Greek poetry.

parody: A humorous literary work that ridicules a serious work by imitating and exaggerating its style.

persona: Refers to a person through whom a fictional narrative is told.

personification: A figure of speech that gives human forms and characteristics to ideas, animals, and other creatures.

plot: The structure of the action of a literary work, rendered and ordered so as to achieve a particular emotional and artistic effect. Some are designed to achieve tragic effects, others to achieve the effects of comedy, romance, or satire. The "story" is the temporal order of events, but plot is how one thing is related to another to achieve effect.

point of view: A phrase used in literary criticism to denote the vantage point from which an author presents the action in a work of fiction (the way a story gets told); includes first, second, and third person, and limited and omniscient points of view. Also, a narrator's perception, interpretation, and evaluation of the matters he narrates may be unreliable or fallible.

protagonist: The chief character in a work (also known as the hero or heroine), on whom our interest centers, and if he or she is pitted against an important opponent, that character is called the antagonist.

puritanism: A religious movement of the sixteenth and seventeenth centuries that sought to "purify" the Church of England. The Puritan's followed the doctrines of John Calvin, and adhered to five basics tenets of religious life: original sin, limited atonement, irresistible grace, perseverance of the saints, and predestination.

realism: A term generally applied to any literature that is true to life, seeking to depict accurately the speech and behavior of ordinary people, and to depict life honestly. It is specifically applied to a movement in the latter half of the 19th century, when novelists were reacting against Romanticism.

regionalist: An author whose writings are closely tied to a particular section of the country.

resolution: How the plot of a story is resolved. Sometimes the resolution my seem artificial, or contrived; other times there may seem to be no resolution at all, which modernists and postmodernists feel better represents reality.

rhetoric: The use of language to influence people emotionally. Frequently, the use of overblown language.

romance: Originally a term denoting a medieval narrative in prose or poetry, dealing with a knightly hero; but now, any fiction concerning heroes, exotic subjects, passionate love, or supernatural experiences.

satire: A literary work making fun of the follies of humanity or society.

sermon: A discourse intended to give spiritual or religious instruction.

setting: In a work of literature it is the general locale, historical time, and social circumstances in which its action occurs.

short story: A brief narrative in prose fiction which introduces a very limited number of characters, with a sustained development of usually only one character; also limited in setting and action.

stigma: A mark of shame or discredit. Stigmata (plural) refers to bodily marks or pains resembling the wounds of the crucified Christ, and sometimes accompanying religious ecstasy.

subplot: A secondary dramatic conflict that runs through a story as a subordinate complication, and which is less important than the main plot.

supernaturalism: Belief in divine or other non-natural influence on human affairs.

symbol: Something, either an object, a person, place, an action, or an idea that is a meaningful entity in itself, and yet stands for, or means, something else. Some symbols are universal or public, others are personal, or have meaning only in the context of a particular story or poem.

theme: Sometimes used interchangeably with "motif," but the term is more usefully applied to a general claim, or doctrine, whether implicit or asserted, which a literary work incorporates. It answers the question, "What is this story about?" It is not the same as the topic, or the subject, but deals with the underlying proposition that the story advances. For example, in the story Redeeming Love, what ultimately is this work saying about the subject of love?

theocracy: A system of government in which the religious leaders are also the political leaders.

tone: The attitude embodied in the language a writer chooses. The tone of a work might be sad, joyful, ironic, solemn, or playful.

tragedy: A serious drama, in prose or poetry, about a person, often of a high station in life, who experiences sudden personal reversals.

transcendentalism: The belief that the visible world, imaginatively and intuitively perceived, provides hints of the invisible, eternal world.

vignette: A brief illustrative story.

Selected Bibliography

Books on Christian Theology in Literature

Begbie, Jeremy, ed. *Beholding the Glory: Incarnation Through the Arts*. Grand Rapids, MI: Baker Books, 2000.

Buechner, Frederick. *Telling the Truth: The Gospel As Tragedy, Comedy & Fairy Tale*. New York: HarperSanFransico/HarperCollins Publishers, 1977.

Gallagher, Susan V. and Roger Lundin. *Literature Through the Eyes of Faith*. Christian College Coalition. HarperSanFrancisco/HarperCollinsPublishers, 1989.

L'Engle, Madeleine. *Walking On Water: Reflections On Faith and Art*. Wheaton, IL: Harold Shaw Publishers, 1980.

Schaeffer, Francis A. *The Complete Works of Francis A. Schaeffer: A Christian Worldview*. Volume Two. "Art in the Bible." *A Christian View of the Bible As Truth*. 2nd ed., 375–413. Westchester, IL: Crossway Books, 1982.

Short, Robert L. "The Church and the Arts." *The Gospel According to Peanuts.*, 7–34 Atlanta: John Knox Press, 1965.

Turner, Steve. *Imagine: A Vision for Christians in the Arts*. Downers Grove, IL: InterVarsity Press, 2001.

Books on Reading Groups (These contain great reading lists)

Jacobsohn, Rachel W. *The Reading Group Handbook*. New York: Hyperion, 1994.

Laskin, David and Holly Hughes. *The Reading Group Book*. New York: Plume/Penguin Books, 1995.

Loevy, Diana. *The Book Club Companion: A Comprehensive Guide to the Reading Group Experience*. New York: Berkley Books, 2006.

McMains, Victoria Golden. *The Reader's Choice: 200 Book Club Favorites*. New York: Quill/HarperCollins, 2000.

Sauer, Patrick. *The Complete Idiot's Guide to Starting a Reading Group*. Idianapolis, IN: alpha books/Macmillan USA, Inc., 2000.

Slezak, Ellen. *The Book Group Book*. 3rd ed. Chicago: Chicago Review Press, 2000.

Other Books That Contain Great Reading Lists

Ayers, Rick and Amy Crawfor, eds. *Great Books for High School Kids: A Teacher's Guide to Books That Can Change Teen's Lives*. Boston: Beacon Press, 2004.

Cowan, Louise and Os Guinness, eds. *Invitation To the Classics*. Grand Rapids, MI: Baker Books, 1998.

The Literary Almanac: The Best of the Printed Word 1900 to the Present. Kansas City: High Tide Press Book/Andrews McMeel Publishing, 1997.

Major, David C. and John S. Major. *100 One-Night Reads: A Book Lover's Guide*. New York: Ballentine Books, 2001.

McKenna, David L. *How to Read a Christian Book*. Grand Rapids, MI: Baker Books, 2001.

Nelson, Sara. *So Many Books So Little Time: A Year of Passionate Reading*. New York: Berkley Books, 2003.

Pearlman, Mickey. *What to Read: The Essential Guide for Reading Group Members and Other Book Lovers*. Revised ed. New York: HarperPerennial/HarperCollins Publishers, 1999.

Petersen, William J. and Randy Petersen. *100 Christian Books That Changed the Century*. Grand Rapids, MI: Baker Books, 2000.

Peterson, Eugene H. *Take and Read: Spiritual Reading, An Annotated List*. Grand Rapids, MI: William B. Eerdmans Publishing Company, 1996.

Rivlin, Holly, and Michael Cavanaugh. *The Barnes & Noble Guide to Children's Books*. New York: Barnes & Noble, 1999.

Strouf, Judie L. H. *Literature Lover's Book of Lists: Serious Trivia For the Bibliophile*. Paramus, NJ: Prentice Hall Press, 1998.

Books About the Reading Life

Corrigan, Maureen. *Leave Me Alone, I'm Reading: Finding and Losing Myself in Books*. New York: Random House, 2005.

Dirda, Michael. *Book by Book: Notes on Reading and Life*. New York: Henry Holt and Company, 2005.

Hunt, Gladys. *Honey For a Woman's Heart: Growing Your World through Reading Great Books*. Grand Rapids, MI: Zondervan, 2002.

Quindlen, Anna. *How Reading Changed My Life*. New York: Library of Contemporary Thought/Ballantine Publishing Group, 1998.

Schwartz, Lynne Sharon. *Ruined By Reading*. Boston: Beacon Press, 1996.

Miscellaneous Books

Karolides, Nicholas J., Margaret Bald, and Dawn B. Sova. *100 Banned Books: Censorship Histories of World Literature*. New York: Checkmark Books/Facts On File, Inc., 1999.

Lewis, C. S. *An Experiment in Criticism*. Cambridge: Cambridge UP, 1961.

Martin, Thomas L., ed. *Reading the Classics With C. S. Lewis*. Grand Rapids, MI: Baker Books, 2000.

Stokes, Penelope J. *The Complete Guide to Writing & Selling the Christian Novel*. Cincinnati, Ohio: Writer's Digest Books, 1998. 1–19.

www.ingramcontent.com/pod-product-compliance
Lightning Source LLC
Chambersburg PA
CBHW060339100426
42812CB00003B/1046